It Is Written...

*Your
Spiritual Sword
&
Shield*

By

DAMMY OWEN

and

OLABISI ODUBANJO

It is Written...
(Your Spiritual Sword and Shield)

Copyright 2009 - Dammy Owen and Olabisi Odubanjo

Printed in the United States of America

ISBN 978-0-9746364-4-9

Printing year 2009

Published by
Elohiym Publishing House
4815 Prince Georges Ave., Suite 204
Beltsville, MD 20705
240-375-8947

Cover Design by: Elohiym Publishing House

All Bible quotations, unless otherwise indicated, are from the (New International Version)
All rights reserved. With the exception of brief exerts used for review purposes, no part of this book may be reproduced or transmitted in any form or by any means, electronic or mechanical, including photocopying, recording, or by any information storage retrieval system, without the written permission from the author.

ORDER ONLINE at or call
www.spiritselect.com
Or www.weomi.org
Tel: 1-(800) 270-9894

DEDICATION

*This book is dedicated to the Father;
who is our Righteous Judge; to Jesus
the owner of the word,;
You are the word itself;
to the Holy Spirit, the helper of our
soul and the power behind every
word of God bringing it
o fulfillment.
To You be glory, honor, and power
forever and ever. Amen,*

ACKNOWLEDGMENT

All Glory and gratitude goes to my Lord and Savior, Jesus Christ; He is the initiator of all things and to Him be all the Glory!

I am grateful to Elohiym Publishing House for the production of this book. This Ministry will continue be be a vessel unto honor in the hand of the Lord Amen! The power of enlargement and the power to make wealth shall be yours; for you shall possess everywhere you place your feet. Amen!

TABLE OF CONTENTS

PAGE

Chapter

	Introduction……………………........…	11
	A Practical Approach………………….	15
	How to Use The Guide ………………….	23
	Authority ……………………….……....	27
2.	Breakthrough…………………………...	31
3.	Breaking Yokes - General………………….	35
4.	Breaking Yokes - Poverty……………….....	41
5.	Casting Out Demonic Spirits…………...........	47
6.	Children …………………….........…………	51
7.	Confusion………………….........…………	55
8.	Curses……………….........…………………	59
9.	Death - Rebuking Death…………………....	61
10.	Establishing faith ……………………........	65
11.	Family Security…………………........………	69
12.	Fear of Attack………………........……………	71
13.	Fear - Anxiety………………………........	75
14.	Fear Of The Unknown ……………………	77
15.	Fear Of Confrontation And Man………………	81
16.	Fear Of Terror…………………........……………	87
17.	Forgiveness from God …………………........	89
18.	Forgiving Others ……………………........	93
19.	Fruit Of The Womb - Barrenness or Delay ……	97

20.	Grieving Hearts	99
21.	Healing - Divine	103
22.	Healing - For the Broken Hearted	109
23.	Marriage	113
24.	Overwhelmed	117
25.	Peace Of God	121
26.	Prosperity - Divine Health	125
27.	Prosperity - Wealth	129
28.	Purpose on Earth	135
29.	Purpose - Ministry	139
30.	Resisting The Devil	143
31.	Resisting Temptation	147
32.	Restoration	151
33.	Safety In Trouble	155
34.	Security	159
35.	Seek to Receive	163
36.	Sleep	167
37.	Sorrow	169
38.	Spirits Leading And Direction	173
39.	Spiritual Attack	177
40.	Vision	183
	A Sample Prayer	187
	About the Authors - *Apostle dammy Owen*	189
	- *Olabisi Odubanjo*	191
	Notes	195

Introduction

" So is my word that goes out from my mouth: It will not return to me empty, but will accomplish what I desire and achieve the purpose for which I sent it."
- Isaiah 55:11

It is a fact that many believers have been praying and fasting with no real result to their prayers. Every thing ordained in the Kingdom of God has a laid out rule, or guideline principle to cause it to manifest in the physical.
Every believer must know how to activate the power of God in prayer; and into every issue that comes along.

As believers, we must know how important the word of God is. We should also know the secret on getting God to appear on the scene of our human needs. The word of God is the same, yesterday, today and forever, and it has been guaranteed with an assurance seal through the Holy Spirit.

"For the word of God is living and active. Sharper than any double-edged sword, it penetrates even to dividing soul and spirit, joints and marrow; it judges the thoughts and attitudes of the heart."
- Hebrews 4:12

God word is law and we receive it through the inspiration of His spirit; and because the words are His, He keeps

watch over every promise within that law to make it good and effective in our lives.
We need to increase our faith so that God can use His words to achieve the miraculous in every situation.

The secret to getting Gods word to become active, is to first believe that no word of God is void of power. The Holy spirit will not move or act until it hears you speak the word of God. When God said *"let there be light"* the Holy Spirit was the one who executed those words.
God watches over every word for healing, deliverance, breakthrough, salvation finances etc.

"The words you speak is a spirit person on its own. The bible said "and the Word was God" - John 1:1

The word of God is Jesus Himself. When you quote the word of God, Jesus manifests in your situation. Believe in every word as you speak it out. ***Have faith!***

Speak the word over and over and it will produce faith in your heart.

As you identify the scriptures for your particular situation; **read the words aloud to activate faith; memorize the word, quote the word in prayer, and digest the word in your heart.** The measure of your faith is proportional to the level or measure of your blessing and miracle.

Just as books stay lifeless on our shelves so can the word of God remain lifeless if not used properly. The power in the word of God is not in you just because you value the Bible as a holy book itself; the word comes into you when you quote the right words in the appropriate situations; aiming to get a definite result.

When you speak the word out in faith, without doubt, you will activate the power within it.

Use the word of God in sincerity and humility with an unshakable mind to declare unto the spiritual world what has already been written concerning your victory over that situation.

Stay Victorious
Apostle Dammy Owen

IT IS WRITTEN ... (YOUR SPIRITUAL SWORD & SHIELD)

A Practical Approach

*"To the law and to the testimony! If they
do not speak according to this word,
they have no light of dawn."*
- Isaiah 8:20

The use of this guide is very simple, but powerful. When you know how to apply the scriptures through prayer you will have become powerful believer whom the devil must stay away from. I want to help you to understand the principle and understanding behind using scriptures to pray.

The things of this earth are a shadow to the things in heaven; we therefore assume then that the system of the law on earth is similar to the in heaven.

We agree that the word of God in the scriptures is law. if it is the law, then we will be judged through these words of God; on the last day when you see Jesus. If the words of the scriptures is law of God, it then means that the words in the scriptures, cover every area of life both on earth as well as in heaven.

The words of God is governed by the courts of heaven and the angels, and on earth we are to be the administrators of it. The conclusion therefore is that there is a system in place which must be followed for the administration of that law *(which is the word of God)*.

*Even now my witness is in heaven;
my advocate is on high."
- Job 16:19*

The Court on Earth
Here on earth, when you want go to court to defend a case or make demand for some rights, you will require an advocate; whether you are represented by an advocate or you choose to represent yourself; you must speak in the language of the court.

The language of the Court
When the advocate stands before the Judge, he will make references to the law, specifying the number, the paragraph and the date of the law; he will then proceed to read the law to the judge; this will bring that particular point to the remembrance of the judge, and it will also allow him to drive home the point at hand.

The law of God is no different. We too have an advocate who is Christ Jesus, He is our mediator and advocate.

*"For there is one God and one mediator
between God and men, the man Christ Jesus"
- 1 Timothy 2:5*

In as much as we have one who is speaking on our behalf, we too have to know what the law says concerning our situation, so that we can bring it to the remembrance of God; especially when we need to make our case before Him.
God says to come reason with Him. He wants you to give him justifiable reason, why He must allow you into His

presence, and to give you what you want.
In the scriptures below; God is already assuming that you will be made clean, if you can come to Him the right way *(After all, He has already made a provision for your cleansing in the word; if you know how to apply it);* to step up boldly to the courts of Heaven and speak up.

> *"Come now, let us reason together," says the LORD.*
> *"Though your sins are like scarlet,*
> *they shall be as white as snow;*
> *though they are red as crimson,*
> *they shall be like wool."*
> *- Isaiah 1:18*

The point here is that; you need to have the word of God that allows you into His presence; you need to know how to clean yourself through the word, and you need to show Him that you know what is written in the law.

"to <u>make her holy</u>, cleansing her by the washing with water through the word" - Ephesians 5:26

Then, He will listen to you and will answer you because He is a righteous God who must always do what is right especially according to his word.

Spiritual Warfare
This same theory applies to spiritual warfare, You nee to make your spiritual stand clear to the devil . The devil only attacks when he knows that you do not know the truth. Lack of knowledge is the weak point of the believer. Everything that we do is taken from and is based on the law of God. The devil knows the law and so does

Jesus. The angels know the law and obey it to the last word; we too are supposed to know the law. The law encompasses, the promises of God, your authority in Christ Jesus, as well as your spiritual weapon by which you can cut through anything. The word of God is a sword and a shield to you.

> *"For the word of God is living and active.*
> *Sharper than any double-edged sword,*
> *<u>it penetrates even to dividing soul</u>*
> *<u>and spirit, joints and marrow;</u>*
> *it judges the thoughts and attitudes of the heart."*
> *- Hebrews 4:12*

When you know the law and you know your right, you will not fear the enemy, nor will you allow the enemy to cheat you, because you know what is yours in the law.
You will not need to beg or argue with God, on any issue; nor will you indulge in pity- parties, lamentations, grumbling and complaining when you know what is available to you.

Jesus using the Word
Jesus set for us an example: When the devil challenged Him after His forty days fasting, Jesus did not need to explain to Him who he was; or why the devil should not bother HIm or ask the devil, with what right he has in challenging the son of God.
Jesus could have kept quite throughout and tell the devil to get behind him. After all, Jesus Himself is the word. From their conversation, it is obvious that the devil knew who He was, but that did not stop him from trying to over-ride God's law.

Jesus simple overcame the enemy by the words of HIs testimony. He testified of what He knew is already written in the law of God. Jesus knows that the things of the spirit are controlled, guided and laid out according to the law . He also knows that the devil knows the law, just as well as He does, so all He needed to do was bring the law to his remembrance; letting him know that he the devil was out of order. The devil took to his heels after that. he never challenged Jesus again.

This same authority has been given to us by Christ Jesus. We just need to know the right law, for the right situation and apply it. The devil will bow and the heavens will be proud of you.

> **[14]Keep reminding them of these things. Warn them before God <u>against quarreling about words; it is of no value,</u> and only ruins those who listen. [15]Do your best to present yourself to God as one approved, a workman who does not need to be ashamed and <u>who correctly handles the word of truth.</u>" - 2 Timothy 2:14-15**

Taking it one Step at a time
Jesus is the author and finisher of our faith and He has set a standard. You cannot become a champion is one day. Take it one day at a time. When you need to pray, open up the scriptures you need in the bible version that suits you, arrange your argument in the way you know it will make sense before a court. You must prove through the scriptures that you must get what ever it is that you need. It is not every prayer that needs this can of procedure , however

when you want something badly, and urgently. make sure it is within the will of God.

Follow this procedure:
1. Prepare your scriptures ahead. Don't overwhelm yourself with too many scriptures.
2. Give thanks unto God, praising His holy name. Praise God who always hears you, especially at the time of your needs. Praise Him for His might to deliver. Praise Him from your heart, until you feel His presence around you.
4. Seek mercy and forgiveness so that nothing will hinder your prayers. *(make sure you are not hindering it yourself; with unforgiveness, bitterness and anger).*
3. Use the verses of scriptures that will establish your relationship with God, concerning your particular issue.
4. Establish your **authority** in Christ through the word with **conviction** in your voice.
5. Begin to declare and decree what must be; through the word, concerning your situation **aggressively.**
6. Begin to ask and thank God for the establishment of His word at this time!
7. Believe every word you have spoken, and begin to thank God for the breakthrough.
8. **Do not doubt.** This means that you should not dwell on that which you have become victorious over in your mind. The devil will bring doubts. The best way to conquer doubt is to pray and leave the issue alone with God. Do not allow your mind to ask you questions if God has done it or not.

believe me! the devil will attempt to cause you to cancel the prayer through doubt. You must keep telling yourself, and I mean speak it aloud; **" God you have done it".** The more you speak it, the more you will believe it.

9. Do not look at the situation either. If the miracle did not manifest immediately, don't doubt; just wait, take your mind off it, and at the time when you have forgotten about it, the Holy Spirit will cause to take note of the issue; for you to see that it is done.

10. Continue to fight, claim or do damage to the kingdom of the devil. The more you pray like this, the more it will become your lifestyle, and before you know it, the scripture verses will all be in your memory and they will come out following like water whenever you need to pray. It is real and it is true. Apply it to yourself!

Concerning this guide:
We have laid out applicable scriptures for you to use in different situations. Not every issue can be covered, and as time goes on, we will update the guide. For now, the basic issues have been covered.

I believe this explanation will help you in some ways. Anyway, if you do not understand how to use the scriptures, you can talk to someone about it or email me at olabisioo@yahoo.com.

May you be empowered through the use of His words in Jesus' name. Amen!

God bless
Olabisi O.

HOW TO USE THE GUIDE

" so is my word that goes out from my mouth: It will not return to me empty, but will accomplish what I desire and achieve the purpose for which I sent it."
- Isaiah 55:11

Read It Out In Prayer!

Read out aloud the verses when praying. Reading them through your mind will do nothing. You have not declared anything; when you read silently. Speak out, so that the angels, the enemy and God; can hear your declarations. They all need to know whether you believe what you are saying. The power of the words of God you speak, is in the way you say it. You are either going to be convincing or be ignored. You need to speak to move someone or get a reaction with those words.

"Truly I tell you, whatever you forbid and declare to be improper and unlawful on earth must be what is already forbidden in heaven, and whatever you permit and declare proper and lawful on earth must be what is already permitted in heaven"
- Matthew 18:18

Speak the words out aloud, memorize them if you can *(at least the ones you use often.)* Continuous use of the same scriptures will cause you to memorize them anyway.

*"You will also declare a thing,
And it will be established for you;
So light will shine on your ways."*
- Job 22:28

This guide is divide into three segments:

1. **Follow Instructions:**
   The first segment may explain how you are to read the scriptures coupled with prayers. This may repeat in some chapters.

2. **Reasoning with God:**
   These are scriptural verses that you bring forth before God, to justify your position, your request, and to remind Him of His promises which must manifest upon your life.

3. **Spiritual Warfare:**
   These are Scriptures for spiritual warfare and they are in two parts. There is attack and there is defense. That is why the scriptures calls it a shield and a Sword. The Sword is to fight and the shield is to defend.

Personalizing Scriptures Verses:

When you quote scriptures, you personalize the verses to you, your family or the person whom the prayer is directed. If you choose not to do this, it is fine, but doing so makes the declaration and of those words that have been personalized more meaningful and effective to the hearer (the ministering angels), and also to you who is speaking the words; it will help you will believe what you are saying.

Scriptures with Power to Demolish the attack of the enemy

IT IS WRITTEN ... (YOUR SPIRITUAL SWORD & SHIELD)

Chapter 1

Authority

Authority to take dominion over issues, over the enemy and audacity to take hold of this authority like a god on earth.

Instructions: All scriptures are taken from New International Version (NIV) Start reading every scripture out aloud with: ***"It is written......"***

SAMPLE VERSE: - "The hands of Zerubbabel have laid the foundation of this temple; his hands will also complete it...."
Read Like This
It is written - "The hands of *(Your Name)* have laid the foundation of this temple; *(My)* hands will also complete it.... "

Declaring Your Stand

It is written..... Genesis 2:19
"........... whatever the man called each living creature, that was its name."

(I therefore take authority to call....)
(You have the authority to rename anything, reject a name or denounce the name of anything especially sickness)

Genesis 9:2
"The fear and dread of you*(me)* will fall upon all the beasts of the earth and all the birds of the air, upon every creature that moves along the ground, and upon all the fish of the sea; they are given into your hands."

Hebrews 13:6
So we *(I) s*ay with confidence, "The Lord is my helper; I will not be afraid. What can man do to me?"

Zechariah 4:9
"The hands of Zerubbabel *(your Name)* have laid the foundation of this temple; his hands will also complete it. Then you will know that the LORD Almighty has sent me to you.

Matthew 18:18
".........., whatever you *(I)* bind on earth will be bound in heaven, and whatever you*(I)* loose on earth will be loosed in heaven.

Matthew 18:19
".......... that if two of you*(us)* on earth agree about anything you ask for, it will be done for you*(us)* by my Father in heaven.

Matthew 18:20
...where two or three come together in my name, there am I*(you are)* with them."

Luke 3:9
The axe is already at the root of the trees, and every tree that does not produce good fruit will be cut down and thrown into the fire."

Luke 10:19

I*(God has)* have given you*(me)* authority to trample on snakes and scorpions and to overcome all the power of the enemy; nothing will harm you*(me)*.

Matthew 17:20

.... if you*(I)* have faith as small as a mustard seed, you can say to this mountain, 'Move from here to there' and it will move. Nothing will be impossible for you*(me)*."

Matthew 21:21-22

.... if you*(I)* have faith and do not doubt, not only can you*(I)* do what was done to the fig tree, but also *(I)* you can say to this mountain, 'Go, throw yourself into the sea,' and it will be done. ²²If you*(I)* believe, you*(I)* will receive whatever you*(I)* ask for in prayer."

Reasoning With God

*It is written.....*Proverbs 21:1
"The king's heart is in the hand of the LORD; he *(you)*directs it like a watercourse wherever he pleases."

Isaiah 44:26

who *(you carry)*carries out the words of his *(your)* servants and fulfills the predictions of his messengers, who says of Jerusalem, 'It shall be inhabited,' of the towns of Judah, 'They shall be built,' and of their ruins, 'I will restore them,'

Spiritual Warfare

It is written..... Romans 14:11
" '........................ 'every knee will bow before me; every tongue will confess to God.'

Isaiah 8:10
"Devise your strategy, but it will be thwarted; propose your plan, but it will not stand, for God is with us.*(me)*"

Philippians 2:10
"that at the name of Jesus every knee should bow, in heaven and on earth and under the earth,

Colossians 2:15
And having disarmed the powers and authorities, he made a public spectacle of them, triumphing over them by the cross.

Revelation 12:11
"They*(I)* overcame him*(you satan)* by the blood of the Lamb and by the word of their*(my)* testimony; they*(I will)* did not love their lives so much as to shrink from death."

Chapter 2

Breakthrough

Breakthrough in every area. Here, you need to talk to God. There is a set time for breakthroughs; and the word will establish you.

Instructions: All scriptures are taken from New International Version (NIV) Start reading every scripture out aloud with: *"It is written......"*

SAMPLE VERSE: - "The hands of Zerubbabel have laid the foundation of this temple; his hands will also complete it...."
Read Like This
It is written - "The hands of *(Your Name)* have laid the foundation of this temple; *(My)* hands will also complete it.... "

Declaring Your Stand

It is written..... **Psalm 102:13**
"You will arise and have compassion on Zion,
for it is time to show favor to her;
the appointed time has come."

Ecclesiastes 8:6
"For there is a proper time and procedure for every
matter, though a man's misery
weighs heavily upon him."

Psalm 25:15
"My eyes are ever on the LORD, for only he will
release my feet from the snare."

Psalm 24:7
"Lift up your heads, O you gates; be lifted up, you ancient doors, that the King of glory may come in."

Psalm 126:5-6
"Those who sow in tears will reap with songs of joy. 6 He who goes out weeping, carrying seed to sow, will return with songs of joy, carrying sheaves with him."

Psalm 127:1
"Unless the LORD builds the house, its builders labor in vain. Unless the LORD watches over the city, the watchmen stand guard in vain."

Joshua 17:18
"... the forested hill country as well. Clear it, and its farthest limits will be yours; though the Canaanites have iron chariots and though they are strong, you can drive them out."

Isaiah 45:3
"I will give you the treasures of darkness, riches stored in secret places, so that you may know that I am the LORD, the God of Israel, who summons you by name."

Isaiah 60:11
"Your gates will always stand open, they will never be shut, day or night, so that men may bring you the wealth of the nations- their kings led in triumphal procession."

Isaiah 61:7
"Instead of their shame my people will receive a double portion, and instead of disgrace they will rejoice in their inheritance; and so they will inherit a double portion in their land, and everlasting joy will be theirs."

Isaiah 62:6-7
"I have posted watchmen on your walls, O Jerusalem; they will never be silent day or night. You who call on the LORD, give yourselves no rest, 7 and give him no rest till he establishes Jerusalem and makes her the praise of the earth."

Zechariah 4:7
"What you, O mighty mountain? Before Zerubbabel you will become level ground. Then he will bring out the capstone to shouts of 'God bless it! God bless it!' "

Zechariah 4:9
"The hands of Zerubbabel have laid the foundation of this temple; his hands will also complete it. Then you will know that the LORD Almighty has sent me to you."

Zechariah 9:11
"As for you, because of the blood of my covenant with you, I will free your prisoners from the waterless pit."

Zechariah 9:12
"Return to your fortress, O prisoners of hope; even now I announce that I will restore twice as much to you."

Matthew 21:21
"Jesus replied, "I tell you the truth, if you have faith and do not doubt, not only can you do what was done to the fig tree, but also you can say to this mountain, 'Go, throw yourself into the sea,' and it will be done."

Matthew 21:22
"If you believe, you will receive whatever you ask for in prayer."

Luke 3:5
"Every valley shall be filled in, every mountain and hill made low. The crooked roads shall become straight, the rough ways smooth"

Isaiah 43:19
"See, I am doing a new thing! Now it springs up; do you not perceive it? I am making a way in the desert and streams in the wasteland."

Chapter 3

Breaking Yokes

Anything that feels like a shackle is a yoke. Declare the power of God to break every yoke. After that, establish your freedom!

Instructions: All scriptures are taken from New International Version (NIV) Start reading every scripture out aloud with: ***"It is written......"***

SAMPLE VERSE: - "The hands of Zerubbabel have laid the foundation of this temple; his hands will also complete it...."
Read Like This
It is written - "The hands of *(Your Name)* have laid the foundation of this temple; *(My)* hands will also complete it.... "

It is written..... Isaiah 43:4
"Since you are precious and honored in my sight, and because I love you, I will give men in exchange for you, and people in exchange for your life."

Psalm 107:16
"for he breaks down gates of bronze and cuts through bars of iron."

Isaiah 9:4
"For as in the day of Midian's defeat, you have shattered the yoke that burdens them, the bar across their shoulders, the rod of their oppressor"

Isaiah 45:2
"I will go before you and will level the mountains; I will break down gates of bronze and cut through bars of iron."

Isaiah 52:2
"Shake off your dust; rise up, sit enthroned, O Jerusalem. Free yourself from the chains on your neck, O captive Daughter of Zion."

Nahum 1:13
"Now I will break their yoke from your neck and tear your shackles away."

Zechariah 9:11
"As for you, because of the blood of my covenant with you, I will free your prisoners from the waterless pit."

2 Corinthians 3:17
"Now the Lord is the Spirit, and where the Spirit of the Lord is, there is freedom."

Colossians 2:15
"And having disarmed the powers and authorities, he made a public spectacle of them, triumphing over them by the cross."

Exodus 6:6
".......... 'I am the LORD, and I will bring you out from under the yoke of the Egyptians. I will free you from being slaves to them, and I will redeem you with an outstretched arm and with mighty acts of judgment."

Luke 3:9
"The axe is already at the root of the trees, and every tree that does not produce good fruit will be cut down and thrown into the fire."

Exodus 6:7
"I will take you as my own people, and I will be your God. Then you will know that I am the LORD your God, who brought you out from under the yoke of the Egyptians."

Leviticus 26:13
"I am the LORD your God, who brought you out of Egypt so that you would no longer be slaves to the Egyptians; I broke the bars of your yoke and enabled you to walk with heads held high."

Isaiah 10:27
"In that day their burden will be lifted from your shoulders, their yoke from your neck; the yoke will be broken because you have grown so fat."

Isaiah 14:25
"I will crush the Assyrian in my land; on my mountains I will trample him down. His yoke will be taken from my people, and his burden removed from their shoulders."

Isaiah 58:6
"It is written..... that you have chosen a fast" ": to loose the chains of injustice and untie the cords of the yoke, to set the oppressed free and break every yoke?"

Ezekiel 34:27
"The trees of the field will yield their fruit and the ground will yield its crops; the people will be secure in their land. They will know that I am the LORD, when I break the bars of their yoke and rescue them from the hands of those who enslaved them."

Hosea 11:4
"I led them with cords of human kindness, with ties of love; I lifted the yoke from their neck and bent down to feed them."

Nahum 1:13
"Now I will break their yoke from your neck and tear your shackles away."

Exodus 40:9
"Take the anointing oil and anoint the tabernacle and everything in it; consecrate it and all its furnishings, and it will be holy."

Psalm 23:5
"You prepare a table before me in the presence of my enemies. You anoint my head with oil;
my cup overflows."

Isaiah 10:27
"And it shall come to pass in that day, that his burden shall be taken away from off thy shoulder, and his yoke from off thy neck, and the yoke shall be destroyed because of the anointing."

Isaiah 14:5
"The LORD has broken the rod of the wicked,
the scepter of the rulers"

Isaiah 28:18
"Your covenant with death will be annulled;
your agreement with the grave will not stand.
When the overwhelming scourge sweeps by,
you will be beaten down by it.

Colossians 2:14-15
"having canceled the written code, with its regulations, that was against us and that stood opposed to us; he took it away, nailing it to the cross. [15]And having disarmed the powers and authorities, he made a public spectacle of them, triumphing over them by the cross.

Isaiah 53:4
"Surely he took up our infirmities and carried our sorrows, yet we considered him stricken by God, smitten by him, and afflicted.

IT IS WRITTEN ... (YOUR SPIRITUAL SWORD & SHIELD)

Chapter 4

Breaking Yokes - Poverty

This yoke is broken in two ways; through the word and through sowing. Sow specific and sacrificial seeds (funds) into the kingdom of God to get a harvest. What you sow is what you will reap! Then, through the word establish the promise of God.

> **Instructions:** All scriptures are taken from New International Version (NIV) Start reading every scripture out aloud with: **"It is written......"**
>
> **SAMPLE VERSE:** - "The hands of Zerubbabel have laid the foundation of this temple; his hands will also complete it...."
> **Read Like This**
> It is written - "The hands of *(Your Name)* have laid the foundation of this temple; *(My)* hands will also complete it.... "

It is written..... Proverbs 23:18
"There is surely a future hope for you, and your hope will not be cut off.

Zechariah 4:9
"The hands of Zerubbabel have laid the foundation of this temple; his hands will also complete it. Then you will know that the LORD Almighty has sent me to you."

Zechariah 9:12
"Return to your fortress, O prisoners of hope; even now I announce that I will restore twice as much to you."

Luke 3:9
"The axe is already at the root of the trees, and every tree that does not produce good fruit will be cut down and thrown into the fire."

2 Corinthians 3:17
"Now the Lord is the Spirit, and where the Spirit of the Lord is, there is freedom."

Psalm 66:12
"You let men ride over our heads; we went through fire and water, but you brought us to a place of abundance."

Psalm 112:3
"Wealth and riches are in his house, and his righteousness endures forever."

Acts 14:17
"Yet he has not left himself without testimony: He has shown kindness by giving you rain from heaven and crops in their seasons; he provides you with plenty of food and fills your hearts with joy."

Proverbs 8:18
" With me are riches and honor, enduring wealth and prosperity."

Ezekiel 34:29
"I will provide for them a land renowned for its crops, and they will no longer be victims of famine in the land or bear the scorn of the nations."

Proverbs 24:4
"And by knowledge shall the chambers be filled with all precious and pleasant riches."

Deuteronomy 28:8
"The LORD will send a blessing on your barns and on everything you put your hand to. The LORD your God will bless you in the land he is giving you."

Psalm 21:3
"You welcomed him with rich blessings and placed a crown of pure gold on his head"

Psalm 128:2
"You will eat the fruit of your labor; blessings and prosperity will be yours."

Proverbs 10:22
"The blessing of the LORD brings wealth, and he adds no trouble to it."

Isaiah 1:19
If you are willing and obedient, you will eat the best from the land;

Isaiah 48:17 (KJV)
"Thus saith the LORD, thy Redeemer, the Holy One of Israel; I am the LORD thy God which teacheth thee to profit, which leadeth thee by the way that thou shouldest go."

Psalm 68:9-11

⁹ "You gave abundant showers, O God; you refreshed your weary inheritance. ¹⁰ Your people settled in it, and from your bounty, O God, you provided for the poor. ¹¹ The Lord announced the word, and great was the company of those who proclaimed it"

Deuteronomy 28:2-4

² "All these blessings will come upon you and accompany you if you obey the LORD your God: ³ You will be blessed in the city and blessed in the country. ⁴ The fruit of your womb will be blessed, and the crops of your land and the young of your livestock-the calves of your herds and the lambs of your flocks."

Deuteronomy 8:18

"......................it is he who gives you the ability to produce wealth, and so confirms his covenant, which he swore to your forefathers, as it is today."

Proverbs 3:16

16 Long life is in her right hand;
in her left hand are riches and honor.

1 Timothy 4:8

"For physical training is of some value, but godliness has value for all things, holding promise for both the present life and the life to come."

Philippians 4: 19
"And my God will meet all your needs according to his glorious riches in Christ Jesus."

Psalm 111:5
"He provides food for those who fear him; he remembers his covenant forever."

IT IS WRITTEN ... (YOUR SPIRITUAL SWORD & SHIELD)

Chapter 5

Casting Out Demonic Spirits

*To cast out evil spirit, you must first establish authority **(CHAPTER 1)** then declare your stand to the enemy.*

Instructions: All scriptures are taken from New International Version (NIV) Start reading every scripture out aloud with: ***"It is written......"***

SAMPLE VERSE: - "The hands of Zerubbabel have laid the foundation of this temple; his hands will also complete it...."
Read Like This
It is written - "The hands of *(Your Name)* have laid the foundation of this temple; *(My)* hands will also complete it.... "

It is written..... Psalm 18:44
"As soon as they hear me, they obey me; foreigners cringe before me."

Psalm 18:45
"They all lose heart; they come trembling from their strongholds. "

Luke 3:9
"The axe is already at the root of the trees, and every tree that does not produce good fruit will be cut down and thrown into the fire."

Matthew 18:18
"I tell you the truth, whatever you bind on earth will be bound in heaven, and whatever you loose on earth will be loosed in heaven."

Luke 10:19
"I have given you authority to trample on snakes and scorpions and to overcome all the power of the enemy; nothing will harm you."

Psalm 24:7
"Lift up your heads, O you gates; be lifted up, you ancient doors, that the King of glory may come in."

Mark 3:15
"And to have power to heal sicknesses, and to cast out devils"

Mark 16:17
"And these signs shall follow them that believe; In my name shall they cast out devils; they shall speak with new tongues"

John 12:31
"Now is the judgment of this world: <u>now</u> shall the prince of this world be cast out."

John 14:12
"..................I tell you the truth, anyone who has faith in me will do what I have been doing. He will do even greater things"

Hebrews 2:14-15

…….. his death he might destroy him who holds the power of death-that is, the devil- 15and free those who all their lives were held in slavery by their fear of death.

Revelation 12:10

10Then I heard a loud voice in heaven say:
"Now have come the salvation and the power and the kingdom of our God, and the authority of his Christ. For the accuser of our brothers, who accuses them before our God day and night, has been hurled down.

Philippians 2:9-11

9Therefore God exalted him to the highest place
and gave him the name that is above every name,
10that at the name of Jesus every knee should bow,
in heaven and on earth and under the earth,
11and every tongue confess that Jesus Christ is Lord,
to the glory of God the Father.

Colossians 2:14-15

14having canceled the written code, with its regulations, that was against us and that stood opposed to us; he took it away, nailing it to the cross. 15And having disarmed the powers and authorities, he made a public spectacle of them, triumphing over them by the cross."

IT IS WRITTEN … (YOUR SPIRITUAL SWORD & SHIELD)

Chapter 6

Children

You need to speak the word of God into your children's lives as seeds that will germinate as they grow.

Instructions: All scriptures are taken from New International Version (NIV) Start reading every scripture out aloud with: *"It is written......"*

SAMPLE VERSE: - "The hands of Zerubbabel have laid the foundation of this temple; his hands will also complete it...."
Read Like This
It is written - "The hands of *(Your Name)* have laid the foundation of this temple; *(My)* hands will also complete it.... "

It is written.....Psalm 112:2
"His children will be mighty in the land; the generation of the upright will be blessed."

Psalm 103:17
But from everlasting to everlasting the LORD's love is with those who fear him, and his righteousness with their children's children-

Psalm 127:3
"Sons are a heritage from the LORD, children a reward from him."

Job 5:25
"You will know that your children will be many, and your descendants like the grass of the earth."

Psalm 8:2
"From the lips of children and infants you have ordained praise because of your enemies, to silence the foe and the avenger."

Psalm 37:25
"I was young and now I am old, yet I have never seen the righteous forsaken or their children begging bread."

Psalm 102:28
"The children of your servants will live in your presence; their descendants will be established before you."

Psalm 37:25
" ……………… I have never seen the righteous forsaken or their children begging bread."

Psalm 90:16
"May your deeds be shown to your servants, your splendor to their children."

Psalm 102:28
"The children of your servants will live in your presence; their descendants will be established before you."

Proverbs 17:6
"Children's children are a crown to the aged, and parents are the pride of their children."

Psalm 127:3
"Sons are a heritage from the LORD, children a reward from him"

Psalm 128:6
"...and may you live to see your children's children."

Proverbs 14:26
"He who fears the LORD has a secure fortress, and for his children it will be a refuge."

Isaiah 8:18
"Here am I, and the children the LORD has given me. We are signs and symbols in Israel from the LORD Almighty, who dwells on Mount Zion."

Isaiah 49:25
"But this is what the LORD says: "Yes, captives will be taken from warriors, and plunder retrieved from the fierce; I will contend with those who contend with you, and your children I will save."

Isaiah 54:13
"All your sons will be taught by the LORD, and great will be your children's peace."

Isaiah 65:23
"They will not toil in vain or bear children doomed to misfortune; for they will be a people blessed by the LORD, they and their descendants with them."

Jeremiah 31:17
"So there is hope for your future," declares the LORD. "Your children will return to their own land."

Matthew 19:14
"............ "Let the little children come to me, and do not hinder them, for the kingdom of heaven belongs to such as these."

Acts 2:39
"The promise is for you and your children and for all who are far off-for all whom the Lord our God will call."

1 John 4:4
"You, dear children, are from God and have overcome them, because the one who is in you is greater than the one who is in the world."

Chapter 7

Confusion

Confusion is a spirit and you need to stand against it, declare what the word of God says concerning your mind.
3 days Fasting and Prayer 6 am - 6 P.M. for God to shed His light is recommended.

Instructions: All scriptures are taken from New International Version (NIV) Start reading every scripture out aloud with: *"It is written......"*

SAMPLE VERSE: - "The hands of Zerubbabel have laid the foundation of this temple; his hands will also complete it...."
Read Like This
It is written - "The hands of *(Your Name)* have laid the foundation of this temple; *(My)* hands will also complete it.... "

It is written..... **Psalm 46:10**
"Be still, and know that I am God; I will be exalted among the nations, I will be exalted in the earth."

Psalm 23:3
"he restores my soul. He guides me in paths of righteousness for his name's sake."

Psalm 112:8
"His heart is secure, he will have no fear; in the end he will look in triumph on his foes"

Psalm 112:4
"Even in darkness light dawns for the upright, for the gracious and compassionate and righteous man."

Isaiah 42:16
"I will lead the blind by ways they have not known,
along unfamiliar paths I will guide them;
I will turn the darkness into light before them
and make the rough places smooth.
These are the things I will do;
I will not forsake them."

Psalm 25:2
"in you I trust, O my God.
Do not let me be put to shame,
nor let my enemies triumph over me."

Psalm 25:4-5
4 "Show me your ways, O LORD,
teach me your paths;
5 guide me in your truth and teach me,
for you are God my Savior, and my hope
is in you all day long."

Psalm 32:8
"I will instruct you and teach you in the way you should go; I will counsel you and watch over you."

Psalm 27
"The LORD is my light and my salvation-whom shall I fear? The LORD is the stronghold of my life of whom shall I be afraid?"

Psalm 27:11
"Teach me your way, O LORD; lead me in a straight path because of my oppressors."

Psalm 27:14
"Wait for the LORD; be strong and take heart and wait for the LORD."

IT IS WRITTEN ... (YOUR SPIRITUAL SWORD & SHIELD)

Chapter 8

Curses

Curses come from disobedience. If the wrong is not made right, nothing will happen. Start out by first using verses for Forgiveness and Mercy, then you will have the stand and authority to break the curses.

> **Instructions:** All scriptures are taken from New International Version (NIV) Start reading every scripture out aloud with: *"It is written......"*
>
> **SAMPLE VERSE:** - "The hands of Zerubbabel have laid the foundation of this temple; his hands will also complete it...."
> **Read Like This**
> It is written - "The hands of *(Your Name)* have laid the foundation of this temple; *(My)* hands will also complete it.... "

It is written..... Luke 3:9
"The axe is already at the root of the trees, and every tree that does not produce good fruit will be cut down and thrown into the fire."

Galatians 3:13
"Christ redeemed us from the curse of the law by becoming a curse for us, for it is written: "Cursed is everyone who is hung on a tree."

Numbers 23:8
"How can I curse those whom God has not cursed? How can I denounce those whom the LORD has not denounced?"

Numbers 24:9
"Like a lion they crouch and lie down, like a lioness who dares to rouse them? "May those who bless you be blessed and those who curse you be cursed!"

Revelation 22:3
"No longer will there be any curse. The throne of God and of the Lamb will be in the city,
and his servants will serve him."

Revelation 5:5
"Then one of the elders said to me, "Do not weep! See, the Lion of the tribe of Judah, the Root of David, has triumphed. He is able to open the scroll
and its seven seals."

Colossians 2:14-15
14having canceled the written code, with its regulations, that was against us and that stood opposed to us; he took it away, nailing it to the cross. 15And having disarmed the powers and authorities, he made a public spectacle of them, triumphing over them by the cross.

Numbers 23:23
"There is no sorcery against Jacob, no divination against Israel. It will now be said of Jacob
and of Israel, 'See what God has done!'

1 John 3:8
"..................... The reason the Son of God appeared was to destroy the devil's work."

Chapter 9

Death
(Rebuking The Spirit of Death and Hades)

Death is a spirit and can invade lives untimely. Stand against if. However, what gives it legal access is sin and disobedience. Seek forgiveness first, and them angrily rebuke the spirit, specifically sending it back to where it came from.

Instructions: All scriptures are taken from New International Version (NIV) Start reading every scripture out aloud with: **"It is written......"**

SAMPLE VERSE: - "The hands of Zerubbabel have laid the foundation of this temple; his hands will also complete it...."
Read Like This
It is written - "The hands of *(Your Name)* have laid the foundation of this temple; *(My)* hands will also complete it.... "

It is written..... Psalm 30:3
"O LORD, you brought me up from the grave; you spared me from going down into the pit."

Psalm 49:15
"But God will redeem my life from the grave; he will surely take me to himself."

Psalm 118:17
"I will not die but live, and will proclaim what the LORD has done."

Psalm 107:20
"He sent forth his word and healed them; he rescued them from the grave."

Psalm 30:9-10
9 "What gain is there in my destruction, in my going down into the pit? Will the dust praise you? Will it proclaim your faithfulness?
10 Hear, O LORD, and be merciful to me; O LORD, be my help."

Psalm 141:8
"But my eyes are fixed on you, O Sovereign LORD; in you I take refuge, do not give me over to death."

Isaiah 38:18
"For the grave cannot praise you, death cannot sing your praise; those who go down to the pit cannot hope for your faithfulness."

Romans 10:13
"for, "Everyone who calls on the name of the Lord will be saved."

Hebrews 11:35
"Women received back their dead, raised to life again. Others were tortured and refused to be released, so that they might gain a better resurrection."

Jude 1:9
"*(satan)*........................."The Lord rebuke you!"

Genesis 15:15
And thou shalt go to thy fathers in peace; thou shalt be buried in a good old age.

Job 21:13
They spend their years in prosperity and go down to the grave in peace.

Psalm 119:25
"I am laid low in the dust; preserve my life according to your word.

Isaiah 28:18a
"Your covenant with death will be annulled; your agreement with the grave will not stand."

1 John 3:8
".......................The reason the Son of God appeared was to destroy the devil's work.

Colossians 2:14-15
14having canceled the written code, with its regulations, that was against us and that stood opposed to us; he took it away, nailing it to the cross. 15And having disarmed the powers and authorities, he made a public spectacle of them, triumphing over them by the cross.

Luke 10:19
"I have given you authority to trample on snakes and scorpions and to overcome all the power of the enemy; nothing will harm you."

Psalm 110:1
" The LORD says to my Lord: "Sit at my right hand until I make your enemies a footstool for your feet."

Psalm 110:2
"The LORD will extend your mighty scepter from Zion; you will rule in the midst of your enemies."

Galatians 2:20
"I have been crucified with Christ and I no longer live, but Christ lives in me. The life I live in the body, I live by faith in the Son of God, who loved me and gave himself for me."

2 Corinthians 5:15
"And he died for all, that those who live should no longer live for themselves but for him who died for them and was raised again."

Hebrews 2:14
"Since the children have flesh and blood, he too shared in their humanity so that by his death he might destroy him who holds the power of death, that is, the devil"

Chapter 10

Establishing Faith

This verses talk to you, to build you up, and when you speak them out, your faith will increase. Use it to pray for others declaring that you believe your prayers. That's Faith!
Speak to yourself and to your situation.

Instructions: All scriptures are taken from New International Version (NIV) Start reading every scripture out aloud with: **"It is written......"**

SAMPLE VERSE: - "The hands of Zerubbabel have laid the foundation of this temple; his hands will also complete it...."
Read Like This
It is written - "The hands of *(Your Name)* have laid the foundation of this temple; *(My)* hands will also complete it.... "

It is written..... Habakkuk 2:4
"........................ the just shall live by his faith."

Matthew 9:29
"..................According to your faith be it unto you."

Matthew 17:20
".................. If ye have faith as a grain of mustard seed, ye shall say unto this mountain, Remove hence to yonder place; and it shall remove; and nothing shall be impossible unto you.

Matthew 21:21
"........................ If ye have faith, and doubt not, ye shall not only do this which is done to the fig tree, but also if ye shall say unto this mountain, Be thou removed, and be thou cast into the sea; it shall be done."

Mark 11:22
"............................. Have faith in God."

Luke 17:6
"........................If ye had faith as a grain of mustard seed, ye might say unto this sycamine tree, Be thou plucked up by the root, and be thou planted in the sea; and it should obey you."

Romans 3:28
"........................... a man is justified by faith without the deeds of the law."

2 Corinthians 5:7
"................For we walk by faith, not by sight"

Ephesians 6:16
"............., taking the shield of faith, wherewith ye shall be able to quench all the fiery darts of the wicked.

Hebrews 11:6
"But without faith it is impossible to please him: for he that cometh to God must believe that he is, and that he is a rewarder of them that diligently seek him."

2 Timothy 4:7
"..................I have fought a good fight, I have finished my course, I have kept the faith"

Hebrews 11:1
"Now faith is the substance of things hoped for, the evidence of things not seen."

James 1:3
"......... that the trying of your faith worketh patience."

James 1:6
"But let him ask in faith, nothing wavering. For he that wavereth is like a wave of the sea driven with the wind and tossed."

James 2:17
"........ faith, if it hath not works, is dead, being alone"

James 2:22
"Seest thou how faith wrought with his works, and by works was faith made perfect?"

1 Peter 1:7
"That the trial of your faith, being much more precious than of gold that perisheth, though it be tried with fire, might be found unto praise and honor and glory at the appearing of Jesus Christ:"

IT IS WRITTEN ... (YOUR SPIRITUAL SWORD & SHIELD)

Chapter 11

Family Security

Declaring the word of God upon yourself and your family will put an edge of protection over them. You cannot have fear in you when you declare these verses. Faith is the key!

Instructions: All scriptures are taken from New International Version (NIV) Start reading every scripture out aloud with: ***"It is written......"***

SAMPLE VERSE: - "The hands of Zerubbabel have laid the foundation of this temple; his hands will also complete it...."
Read Like This
It is written - "The hands of *(Your Name)* have laid the foundation of this temple; *(My)* hands will also complete it.... "

It is written..... Psalm 91:9-10
9 If you make the Most High your dwelling- even the LORD, who is my refuge- 10 then no harm will befall you, no disaster will come near your tent.

Isaiah 8:18
"Here am I, and the children the LORD has given me. We are signs and symbols in Israel from the LORD Almighty, who dwells on Mount Zion."

Matthew 21:22
"If you believe, you will receive whatever you ask for in prayer."

Galatians 6:17
"Finally, let no one cause me trouble, for I bear on my body the marks of Jesus."

Deuteronomy 33:12
"..............."Let the beloved of the LORD rest secure in him, for he shields him all day long, and the one the LORD loves rests between his shoulders."

Job 5:24
"You will know that your tent is secure; you will take stock of your property and find nothing missing."

Job 11:18
"You will be secure, because there is hope; you will look about you and take your rest in safety"

Psalm 16:5
"LORD, you have assigned me my portion and my cup; you have made my lot secure."

Galatians 5:10
"I am confident in the Lord that you will take no other view. The one who is throwing you into confusion will pay the penalty, whoever he may be."

Proverbs 2:21
21 For the upright will live in the land,
and the blameless will remain in it;

Chapter 12

Fear - Attack

Any attack must be handled in Holy anger. Declare to the enemy and let him understand that God has not given you a spirit of fear! He is only wasting time. Speak the words he understands.

Instructions: All scriptures are taken from New International Version (NIV) Start reading every scripture out aloud with: *"It is written......"*

SAMPLE VERSE: - "The hands of Zerubbabel have laid the foundation of this temple; his hands will also complete it...."
Read Like This
It is written - "The hands of *(Your Name)* have laid the foundation of this temple; *(My)* hands will also complete it.... "

It is written..... Psalm 94:22
"But the LORD has become my fortress, and my God the rock in whom I take refuge."

Psalm 27:1
"The LORD is my light and my salvation-whom shall I fear? The LORD is the stronghold of my life-of whom shall I be afraid?

Psalm 3:6
"I will not fear the tens of thousands drawn up against me on every side."

Isaiah 49:25
"But this is what the LORD says: "Yes, captives will be taken from warriors, and plunder retrieved from the fierce; I will contend with those who contend with you, and your children I will save."

Revelation 12:11
"They overcame him by the blood of the Lamb and by the word of their testimony; they did not love their lives so much as to shrink from death."

Deuteronomy 3:22
Do not be afraid of them; the LORD your God himself will fight for you."

2 Chronicles 20:15
" .... This is what the LORD says to you: 'Do not be afraid or discouraged because of this vast army. For the battle is not yours, but God's."

2 Chronicles 20:17
"You will not have to fight this battle. Take up your positions; stand firm and see the deliverance the LORD will give you, O Judah and Jerusalem. Do not be afraid; do not be discouraged. Go out to face them tomorrow, and the LORD will be with you.' "

Numbers 14:9
" .... Their protection is gone, but the LORD is with us. Do not be afraid of them."

Deuteronomy 31:6
"Be strong and courageous. Do not be afraid or terrified because of them, for the LORD your God goes with you; he will never leave you nor forsake you."

Deuteronomy 31:8
"The LORD himself goes before you and will be with you; he will never leave you nor forsake you. Do not be afraid; do not be discouraged."

Deuteronomy 20:4
"For the LORD your God is the one who goes with you to fight for you against your enemies to give you victory."

Joshua 23:10
"One of you routs a thousand, because the LORD your God fights for you, just as he promised.

Joshua 23:9
"The LORD has driven out before you great and powerful nations; to this day no one has been able to withstand you."

Hebrews 13:5-6
5"............................."Never will I leave you; never will I forsake you. 6So we say with confidence, "The Lord is my helper; I will not be afraid. What can man do to me?"

Psalm 34:5-6
⁵ Those who look to him are radiant;
their faces are never covered with shame.
⁶ This poor man called, and the LORD heard him;
he saved him out of all his troubles.

Psalm 34:7
"The angel of the LORD encamps around those who fear him, and he delivers them."

Psalm 28:8
"The LORD is the strength of his people, a fortress of salvation for his anointed one.

Psalm 27:3
"Though an army besiege me, my heart will not fear; though war break out against me, even then will I be confident."

Psalm 20:6
"Now I know that the LORD saves his anointed; he answers him from his holy heaven with the saving power of his right hand."

Psalm 16:8
"I have set the LORD always before me. Because he is at my right hand, I will not be shaken."

Chapter 13

Fear - Anxiety

Shake off anxiety. It is not of God. It is an evil sprit sent to take you out of God's presence. Declare to the enemy and let him understand that God has not given you a spirit of fear! You will seek the peace of God.. Speak the words he understands.

Instructions: All scriptures are taken from New International Version (NIV) Start reading every scripture out aloud with: ***"It is written......"***

SAMPLE VERSE: - "The hands of Zerubbabel have laid the foundation of this temple; his hands will also complete it...."
Read Like This
It is written - "The hands of *(Your Name)* have laid the foundation of this temple; *(My)* hands will also complete it.... "

It is written.....Psalm 112:7
"He will have no fear of bad news; his heart is steadfast, trusting in the LORD."

Jeremiah 31:16
"This is what the LORD says: "Restrain your voice from weeping and your eyes from tears, for your work will be rewarded," declares the LORD...."

Matthew 21:21
"................. if you have faith and do not doubt, not only can you do what was done to the fig tree, but also you can say to this mountain, 'Go, throw yourself into the sea,' and it will be done."

2 Corinthians 3:17
"Now the Lord is the Spirit, and where the Spirit of the Lord is, there is freedom."

1 Peter 4:7
"The end of all things is near. Therefore be clear minded and self-controlled so that you can pray."

Deuteronomy 31:8
"The LORD himself goes before you and will be with you; he will never leave you nor forsake you. Do not be afraid; do not be discouraged."

Chapter 14

Fear Of the Unknown

Only the words of God can penetrate through to the spirit of fear,r especially when you do not know why you are fearful.
Rebuke it and be free!

Instructions: All scriptures are taken from New International Version (NIV) Start reading every scripture out aloud with: ***"It is written......"***

SAMPLE VERSE: - "The hands of Zerubbabel have laid the foundation of this temple; his hands will also complete it...."
Read Like This
It is written - "The hands of *(Your Name)* have laid the foundation of this temple; *(My)* hands will also complete it.... "

It is written..... Psalm 46:1
"God is our refuge and strength, an ever-present help in trouble."

Psalm 23:4
"Even though I walk through the valley of the shadow of death, I will fear no evil, for you are with me; your rod and your staff, they comfort me. "

Psalm 118:5
" In my anguish I cried to the LORD, and he answered by setting me free."

Psalm 56:3-4

³"When I am afraid, I will trust in you. ⁴ In God, whose word I praise, in God I trust; I will not be afraid. What can mortal man do to me?"

Psalm 118:6-7

⁶"The LORD is with me; I will not be afraid. What can man do to me? ⁷ The LORD is with me; he is my helper. I will look in triumph on my enemies."

Psalm 25:3

"No one whose hope is in you will ever be put to shame, but they will be put to shame who are treacherous without excuse.

Ezekiel 2:6

".............. do not be afraid of them or their words. Do not be afraid, though briers and thorns are all around you and you live among scorpions.
Do not be afraid of what they say or terrified by them, though they are a rebellious house."

Romans 10:13

"for, "Everyone who calls on the name of the Lord will be saved.""

Job 39:22

"He laughs at fear, afraid of nothing; he does not shy away from the sword."

Isaiah 41:14
"Do not be afraid, O worm Jacob, O little Israel, for I myself will help you," declares the LORD, your Redeemer, the Holy One of Israel."

Isaiah 44:2
"This is what the LORD says- he who made you, who formed you in the womb, and who will help you: Do not be afraid, O Jacob, my servant, Jeshurun, whom I have chosen"

Isaiah 54:4
"Do not be afraid; you will not suffer shame. Do not fear disgrace; you will not be humiliated. You will forget the shame of your youth and remember no more the reproach of your widowhood."

Jeremiah 1:8
"Do not be afraid of them, for I am with you and will rescue you," declares the LORD."

Zechariah 8:13
"As you have been an object of cursing among the nations, O Judah and Israel, so will I save you, and you will be a blessing. Do not be afraid, but let your hands be strong."

IT IS WRITTEN ... (YOUR SPIRITUAL SWORD & SHIELD)

Chapter 15

Fear Of Confrontation

This is the fear of man. It is a snare! Speak the word to reject it and stand firm, unafraid of any consequences. The Lord is by your side. Declare the word to yourself and the situation in prayer.

Instructions: All scriptures are taken from New International Version (NIV) Start reading every scripture out aloud with: *"It is written......"*

SAMPLE VERSE: - "The hands of Zerubbabel have laid the foundation of this temple; his hands will also complete it...."
Read Like This
It is written - "The hands of *(Your Name)* have laid the foundation of this temple; *(My)* hands will also complete it.... "

It is written.....Psalm 68:1
"May God arise, may his enemies be scattered; may his foes flee before him."

Psalm 16:8
"I have set the LORD always before me. Because he is at my right hand, I will not be shaken."

Isaiah 50:7
"Because the Sovereign LORD helps me, I will not be disgraced. Therefore have I set my face like flint, and I know I will not be put to shame."

Psalm 27:2-3

2 "When evil men advance against me to devour my flesh, [a] when my enemies and my foes attack me, they will stumble and fall. 3 Though an army besiege me, my heart will not fear; though war break out against me, even then will I be confident."

Exodus 14:13

"...................., "Do not be afraid. Stand firm and you will see the deliverance the LORD will bring you today. The Egyptians you see today you will never see again.

Isaiah 54:14

"In righteousness you will be established: Tyranny will be far from you; you will have nothing to fear. Terror will be far removed; it will not come near you."

Hebrews 13:6

"So we say with confidence, "The Lord is my helper; I will not be afraid. What can man do to me?"

2 Kings 6:16

"Don't be afraid," the prophet answered. "Those who are with us are more than those who are with them."

2 Chronicles 20:17

"You will not have to fight this battle. Take up your positions; stand firm and see the deliverance the LORD will give you, O Judah and Jerusalem. Do not be afraid; do not be discouraged. Go out to face them tomorrow, and the LORD will be with you.' "

Psalm 27:1
"The LORD is my light and my salvation- whom shall I fear? The LORD is the stronghold of my life- of whom shall I be afraid?"

Psalm 56:3
"When I am afraid, I will trust in you."

Isaiah 7:4
"Say to him, 'Be careful, keep calm and don't be afraid. Do not lose heart because of these two smoldering stubs of firewood."

Isaiah 44:8
"Do not tremble, do not be afraid. Did I not proclaim this and foretell it long ago? You are my witnesses. Is there any God besides me? No, there is no other Rock; I know not one."

Hebrews 13:6
"So we say with confidence, "The Lord is my helper; I will not be afraid. What can man do to me?"

Job 5:21
"You will be protected from the lash of the tongue, and need not fear when destruction comes."

Job 3:25
"What I feared has come upon me; what I dreaded has happened to me."

Job 5:22
"You will laugh at destruction and famine, and need not fear the beasts of the earth."

Job 11:15
".. you will lift up your face without shame; you will stand firm and without fear."

Job 21:9
"Their homes are safe and free from fear; the rod of God is not upon them."

Psalm 3:6
"I will not fear the tens of thousands drawn up against me on every side"

Psalm 34:4
"I sought the LORD, and he answered me; he delivered me from all my fears."

Psalm 46:2
"Therefore we will not fear, though the earth give way and the mountains fall into the heart of the sea,"

Psalm 91:5
"You will not fear the terror of night, nor the arrow that flies by day"

Psalm 112:7
"He will have no fear of bad news; his heart is steadfast, trusting in the LORD."

Psalm 112:8
"His heart is secure, he will have no fear; in the end he will look in triumph on his foes"

Proverbs 3:25
"Have no fear of sudden disaster or of the ruin that overtakes the wicked"

Proverbs 29:25
"Fear of man will prove to be a snare, but whoever trusts in the LORD is kept safe."

Isaiah 8:12
"Do not call conspiracy everything that these people call conspiracy ; do not fear what they fear, and do not dread it."

Isaiah 41:13
"For I am the LORD, your God, who takes hold of your right hand and says to you, Do not fear; I will help you."

Isaiah 43:1
"But now, this is what the LORD says- he who created you, O Jacob, he who formed you, O Israel: "Fear not, for I have redeemed you; I have summoned you by name; you are mine."

Jeremiah 10:5
"Like a scarecrow in a melon patch, their idols cannot speak; they must be carried because they cannot walk. Do not fear them; they can do no harm nor can they do any good."

Jeremiah 30:10

" 'So do not fear, O Jacob my servant; do not be dismayed, O Israel,' declares the LORD. 'I will surely save you out of a distant place, your descendants from the land of their exile. Jacob will again have peace and security, and no one will make him afraid."

1 John 4:18

"There is no fear in love. But perfect love drives out fear, because fear has to do with punishment. The one who fears is not made perfect in love."

1 Peter 3:14

"But even if you should suffer for what is right, you are blessed. "Do not fear what they fear ;
do not be frightened."

Chapter 16

Fear Of Terror

Terror and terrorist go together. What God has given us is peace. Declare the word to establish your position in God.

> **Instructions:** All scriptures are taken from New International Version (NIV) Start reading every scripture out aloud with: ***"It is written......"***
>
> **SAMPLE VERSE:** - "The hands of Zerubbabel have laid the foundation of this temple; his hands will also complete it...."
> **Read Like This**
> It is written - "The hands of *(Your Name)* have laid the foundation of this temple; *(My)* hands will also complete it...."

It is written..... Psalm 91:3
"Surely he will save you from the fowler's snare and from the deadly pestilence."

Isaiah 8:12
"Do not call conspiracy everything that these people call conspiracy; do not fear what they fear, and do not dread it."

Psalm 121:7
" The LORD will keep you from all harm-he will watch over your life"

Job 5:22
"You will laugh at destruction and famine, and need not fear the beasts of the earth."

Joshua 1:9
"Have I not commanded you? Be strong and courageous. Do not be terrified; do not be discouraged, for the LORD your God will be with you wherever you go."

Matthew 10:31
"So don't be afraid; you are worth more than many sparrows."

John 14:27
"Peace I leave with you; my peace I give you. I do not give to you as the world gives. Do not let your hearts be troubled and do not be afraid."

2 Chronicles 20:15
"............'Do not be afraid or discouraged because of this vast army. For the battle is not yours, but God's. "

Isaiah 12:2
"Surely God is my salvation; I will trust and not be afraid. The LORD, the LORD, is my strength and my song; he has become my salvation."

Isaiah 44:8
"Do not tremble, do not be afraid. Did I not proclaim this and foretell it long ago? You are my witnesses. Is there any God besides me? No, there is no other Rock; I know not one."

Chapter 17

Forgiveness and Mercy

*This is a chapter that is needed before any prayer and the use of it should be daily or as often as is needed.
Every form of bondage is caused by sin and disobedience.
Forgiveness and Mercy of God must first be established before freedom and restoration*

> **Instructions:** All scriptures are taken from New International Version (NIV) Start reading every scripture out aloud with: ***"It is written......"***
>
> **SAMPLE VERSE:** - "The hands of Zerubbabel have laid the foundation of this temple; his hands will also complete it...."
> **Read Like This**
> **It is written** - "The hands of *(Your Name)* have laid the foundation of this temple; *(My)* hands will also complete it.... "

It is written..... Psalm 19:14
"May the words of my mouth and the meditation of my heart be pleasing in your sight, O LORD, my Rock and my Redeemer."

Psalm 30:5
"For his anger lasts only a moment, but his favor lasts a lifetime; weeping may remain for a night, but rejoicing comes in the morning."

Psalm 25:11
"For the sake of your name, O LORD, forgive my iniquity, though it is great."

Psalm 103:8-10

⁸ "The LORD is compassionate and gracious, slow to anger, abounding in love.
⁹ He will not always accuse, nor will he harbor his anger forever; 10 he does not treat us as our sins deserve or repay us according to our iniquities."

2 Samuel 24:14

"..................... Let us fall into the hands of the LORD, for his mercy is great; but do not let me fall into the hands of men."

1 Kings 8:30

"Hear the supplication of your servant and of your people Israel when they pray toward this place. Hear from heaven, ...and when you hear, forgive."

Psalm 19:12

"Who can discern his errors? Forgive my hidden faults."

Psalm 25:11

"For the sake of your name, O LORD, forgive my iniquity, though it is great."

Ephesians 1:7

"In him we have redemption through his blood, the forgiveness of sins, in accordance with the riches of God's grace"

Psalm 32:1
"Blessed is he whose transgressions are forgiven, whose sins are covered."

Psalm 79:9
"Help us, O God our Savior, for the glory of your name; deliver us and forgive our sins for your name's sake. "

Psalm 103:3
"....who forgives all your sins and heals all your diseases"

Psalm 130:4
"But with you there is forgiveness; therefore you are feared."

Jeremiah 33:8
"I will cleanse them from all the sin they have committed against me and will forgive all their sins of rebellion against me."

Mark 3:28
"I tell you the truth, all the sins and blasphemies of men will be forgiven them."

Psalm 51:7
"Purge me with hyssop *(the Blood of Jesus)*, and I shall be clean;
Wash me, and I shall be whiter than snow."

Read the whole of **Psalm 51** and **Psalm 32**

IT IS WRITTEN ... (YOUR SPIRITUAL SWORD & SHIELD)

Chapter 18

Forgiving Others

Unforgiveness is a hindrance to prayer and breakthroughs. It is also hard to let go, except through the word of God. Use the word to cleanse your heart!

Instructions: All scriptures are taken from New International Version (NIV) Start reading every scripture out aloud with: **"It is written......"**

SAMPLE VERSE: - "The hands of Zerubbabel have laid the foundation of this temple; his hands will also complete it...."
Read Like This
It is written - "The hands of *(Your Name)* have laid the foundation of this temple; *(My)* hands will also complete it...."

It is written..... Isaiah 43:18-19
18 "Forget the former things; do not dwell on the past.
19 See, I am doing a new thing!
Now it springs up; do you not perceive it? I am making a way in the desert and streams in the wasteland"

James 1:19
"See, I am doing a new thing! Now it springs up; do you not perceive it? I am making a way in the desert and streams in the wasteland"

Matthew 6:12
"Forgive us our debts, as we also have forgiven our debtors."

Matthew 6:14-15
"For if you forgive men when they sin against you, your heavenly Father will also forgive you. But if you do not forgive men their sins, your Father will not forgive your sins."

Matthew 18:35
"This is how my heavenly Father will treat each of you unless you forgive your brother from your heart."

Matthew 26:28
"This is my blood of the covenant, which is poured out for many for the forgiveness of sins."

Mark 11:25
"And when you stand praying, if you hold anything against anyone, forgive him, so that your Father in heaven may forgive you your sins."

Luke 6:37
"Do not judge, and you will not be judged. Do not condemn, and you will not be condemned. Forgive, and you will be forgiven."

Luke 11:4
"Forgive us our sins, for we also forgive everyone who sins against us. And lead us not into temptation.' "

Luke 17:3
"So watch yourselves. "If your brother sins, rebuke him, and if he repents, forgive him."

John 20:23
"If you forgive anyone his sins, they are forgiven; if you do not forgive them, they are not forgiven."

Acts 26:18
"..........to open their eyes and turn them from darkness to light, and from the power of Satan to God, so that they may receive forgiveness of sins and a place among those who are sanctified by faith in me.'

2 Corinthians 2:7
"Now instead, you ought to forgive and comfort him, so that he will not be overwhelmed by excessive sorrow. "

Colossians 3:13
"Bear with each other and forgive whatever grievances you may have against one another. Forgive as the Lord forgave you."

James 5:15
"And the prayer offered in faith will make the sick person well; the Lord will raise him up. If he has sinned, he will be forgiven."

1 John 1:9
"If we confess our sins, he is faithful and just and will forgive us our sins and purify us from all unrighteousness."

IT IS WRITTEN ... (YOUR SPIRITUAL SWORD & SHIELD)

Chapter 19

Fruit Of The Womb

There is power in declaring what is rightfully yours. Before this declarations, seek to find the root cause of the problem. The devil is hiding somewhere! Pray accordingly to break any demonic hindrances first, then go on to receive as you have declared!

Instructions: All scriptures are taken from New International Version (NIV) Start reading every scripture out aloud with: **"It is written......"**

SAMPLE VERSE: - "The hands of Zerubbabel have laid the foundation of this temple; his hands will also complete it...."
Read Like This
It is written - "The hands of *(Your Name)* have laid the foundation of this temple; *(My)* hands will also complete it.... "

It is written..... Deuteronomy 28:11
"The LORD will grant you abundant prosperity-in the fruit of your womb, the young of your livestock and the crops of your ground-in the land he swore to your forefathers to give you."

Deuteronomy 28:4
"The fruit of your womb will be blessed, and the crops of your land and the young of your livestock-the calves of your herds and the lambs of your flocks."

Psalm 113:9
"He settles the barren woman in her home as a happy mother of children. Praise the LORD"

Psalm 128:3
"Your wife will be like a fruitful vine within your house; your sons will be like olive shoots around your table.

Exodus 23:25-26
25 "Worship the LORD your God, and his blessing will be on your food and water. I will take away sickness from among you, 26 and none will miscarry or be barren in your land. I will give you a full life span"

Isaiah 54:1
"Sing, O barren woman, you who never bore a child; burst into song, shout for joy, you who were never in labor; because more are the children of the desolate woman than of her who has a husband," says the LORD."

Zechariah 9:9
"Rejoice greatly, O Daughter of Zion! Shout, Daughter of Jerusalem! See, your king comes to you, righteous and having salvation, gentle and riding on a donkey, on a colt, the foal of a donkey. "

Philippians 4:19
"And my God will meet all your needs according to his glorious riches in Christ Jesus."

Genesis 9:1
"Then God blessed Noah and his sons, saying to them, "Be fruitful and increase in number and fill the earth."

Chapter 20

Grieving Hearts

Reading and meditating on these words of God will bring light when you are grieving. It is a sure medicine!

Instructions: All scriptures are taken from New International Version (NIV) Start reading every scripture out aloud with: **"It is written......"**

SAMPLE VERSE: - "The hands of Zerubbabel have laid the foundation of this temple; his hands will also complete it...."
Read Like This
It is written - "The hands of *(Your Name)* have laid the foundation of this temple; *(My)* hands will also complete it.... "

It is written..... Isaiah 57:1
"The righteous perish, and no one ponders it in his heart; devout men are taken away, and no one understands that the righteous are taken away to be spared from evil."

2 Corinthians 12:9
"......... "My grace is sufficient for you, for my power is made perfect in weakness." Therefore I will boast all the more gladly about my weaknesses, so that Christ's power may rest on me."

Colossians 1:17
"He is before all things, and in him all things hold together."

Romans 8:28
"And we know that in all things God works for the good of those who love him, who have been called according to his purpose."

Nehemiah 8:10
".......... "Go and enjoy choice food and sweet drinks, and send some to those who have nothing prepared. This day is sacred to our Lord. Do not grieve, for the joy of the LORD is your strength."

Isaiah 61:3
"..provide for those who grieve in Zion, to bestow on them a crown of beauty instead of ashes,
the oil of gladness instead of mourning, and a garment of praise instead of a spirit of despair.
They will be called oaks of righteousness, a planting of the LORD for the display of his splendor.

1 Thessalonians 4:13
"Brothers, we do not want you to be ignorant about those who fall asleep, or to grieve like the rest of men, who have no hope."

2 Corinthians 9:8
"And God is able to make all grace abound to you, so that in all things at all times, having all that you need, you will abound in every good work."

Philippians 4:13
"I can do everything through him who gives me strength."

Psalm 30:11-12

¹¹"You turned my wailing into dancing; you removed my sackcloth and clothed me with joy,
¹² that my heart may sing to you and not be silent. O LORD my God, I will give you thanks forever.

Isaiah 12:1

" In that day you will say:
"I will praise you, O LORD.
Although you were angry with me,
your anger has turned away
and you have comforted me."

Psalm 12:1

"Help, LORD, for the godly are no more;
the faithful have vanished from among men."

John 14:1

"Do not let your hearts be troubled. Trust in God; trust also in me.

Jeremiah 20:11

" But the LORD is with me like a mighty warrior;
so my persecutors will stumble and not prevail.
They will fail and be thoroughly disgraced;
their dishonor will never be forgotten."

Isaiah 40:31

"but those who hope in the LORD will renew their strength. They will soar on wings like eagles;
they will run and not grow weary,
they will walk and not be faint."

Isaiah 41:10

"So do not fear, for I am with you;
do not be dismayed, for I am your God.
I will strengthen you and help you;
I will uphold you with my righteous right hand."

Psalm 121:1

"I lift up my eyes to the hills-
where does my help come from?"

Psalm 116:3-4

3 "The cords of death entangled me,
the anguish of the grave [a] came upon me;
I was overcome by trouble and sorrow.
4 Then I called on the name of the LORD :
"O LORD, save me!"

Psalm 116:7

"Be at rest once more, O my soul,
for the LORD has been good to you."

Chapter 21

Healing - Divine

Divine healing is seeking immediate healing. quoting the scripture frequently despatches arrow of fire at the enemy. However seek forgiveness first. Sickness will most times come from sin and disobedience.

Instructions: All scriptures are taken from New International Version (NIV) Start reading every scripture out aloud with: ***"It is written......"***

SAMPLE VERSE: - "The hands of Zerubbabel have laid the foundation of this temple; his hands will also complete it...."
Read Like This
It is written - "The hands of *(Your Name)* have laid the foundation of this temple; *(My)* hands will also complete it.... "

It is written..... James 5:15
"And the prayer offered in faith will make the sick person well; the Lord will raise him up. If he has sinned, he will be forgiven."

Romans 10:13
"for, "Everyone who calls on the name of the Lord will be saved."

Matthew 18:19
"Again, I tell you that if two of you on earth agree about anything you ask for, it will be done for you by my Father in heaven."

Exodus 15:26
... "If you listen carefully to the voice of the LORD your God and do what is right in his eyes, if you pay attention to his commands and keep all his decrees, I will not bring on you any of the diseases I brought on the Egyptians, for I am the LORD, who heals you."

Jude 1:9
………………………….."The Lord rebuke you!"

2 Peter 3:9
"The Lord is not slow in keeping his promise, as some understand slowness. He is patient with you, not wanting anyone to perish, but everyone to come to repentance"

2 Peter 1:3
³His divine power has given us everything we need for life and godliness through our knowledge of him who called us by his own glory and goodness"

Isaiah 53:4
"Surely he took up our infirmities and carried our sorrows, yet we considered him stricken by God, smitten by him, and afflicted."

Malachi 4:2
"But for you who revere my name, the sun of righteousness will rise with healing in its wings. And you will go out and leap like calves released from the stall."

2 Kings 20:5
" 'This is what the LORD, the God of your father David, says: I have heard your prayer and seen your tears; I will heal you."

Psalm 30:2
"O LORD my God, I called to you for help and you healed me."

Psalm 103:3
".......who forgives all your sins and heals all your diseases,

Psalm 107:20
"He sent forth his word and healed them; he rescued them from the grave."

Isaiah 38:16
"Lord, by such things men live; and my spirit finds life in them too. You restored me to health and let me live."

Jeremiah 17:14
"Heal me, O LORD, and I will be healed; save me and I will be saved, for you are the one I praise."

Jeremiah 30:17
"But I will restore you to health and heal your wounds,' declares the LORD, 'because you are called an outcast, Zion for whom no one cares."

Jeremiah 33:6
" 'Nevertheless, I will bring health and healing to it; I will heal my people and will let them enjoy abundant peace and security."

Revelation 12:11
"They overcame him by the blood of the Lamb and by the word of their testimony; they did not love their lives so much as to shrink from death."

Matthew 7:19
"Every tree that does not bear good fruit is cut down and thrown into the fire."

2 Corinthians 9:8
"And God is able to make all grace abound to you"

Psalm 18:6
"In my distress I called to the LORD; I cried to my God for help. From his temple he heard my voice; my cry came before him, into his ears."

1 Samuel 25:6
"Say to him: 'Long life to you! Good health to you and your household! And good health to all that is yours!"

Psalm 147:3
"He heals the brokenhearted and binds up their wounds."

Proverbs 4:22
22 for they are life to those who find them and health to a man's whole body.

Isaiah 53:5
5 But he was pierced for our transgressions, he was crushed for our iniquities; the punishment that brought us peace was upon him,
and by his wounds we are healed.

Exodus 23:25-26
25 "Worship the LORD your God, and his blessing will be on your food and water. I will take away sickness from among you, 26 and none will miscarry or be barren in your land. I will give you a full life span.

Psalm 103:3
"who forgives all your sins and heals all your diseases,

Philippians 4:19
"And my God will meet all your needs according to his glorious riches in Christ Jesus."

John 14:14
"You may ask me for anything in my name, and I will do it."

IT IS WRITTEN ... (YOUR SPIRITUAL SWORD & SHIELD)

Chapter 22

Healing - For the Broken Hearted

Declare these words to yourself or to one who needs to feel the love of God around them and within them. The words will penetrate to their souls and marrows for healing.

> **Instructions:** All scriptures are taken from New International Version (NIV) Start reading every scripture out aloud with: ***"It is written......"***
>
> <u>SAMPLE VERSE:</u> - "The hands of Zerubbabel have laid the foundation of this temple; his hands will also complete it...."
> **Read Like This**
> **It is written** - "The hands of *(Your Name)* have laid the foundation of this temple; *(My)* hands will also complete it.... "

It is written..... Psalm 34:18
"The LORD is close to the brokenhearted and saves those who are crushed in spirit."

2 Corinthians 12:9
"............ "My grace is sufficient for you, for my power is made perfect in weakness." Therefore I will boast all the more gladly about my weaknesses, so that Christ's power may rest on me."

1 Peter 4:7
"The end of all things is near. Therefore be clear minded and self-controlled so that you can pray."

Revelation 12:11
"They overcame him by the blood of the Lamb and by the word of their testimony; they did not love their lives so much as to shrink from death.

Isaiah 61:1
"The Spirit of the Lord GOD is upon me; because the LORD hath anointed me to preach good tidings unto the meek; he hath sent me to bind up the brokenhearted, to proclaim liberty to the captives, and the opening of the prison to them that are bound;"

Romans 8:1
"Therefore, there is now no condemnation for those who are in Christ Jesus:"

Ephesians 4:24
"and to put on the new self, created to be like God in true righteousness and holiness."

2 Peter 1:4
"Through these he has given us his very great and precious promises, so that through them you may participate in the divine nature and escape the corruption in the world caused by evil desires."

Romans 8:34
"Who is he that condemns? Christ Jesus, who died-more than that, who was raised to life-is at the right hand of God and is also interceding for us."

Philippians 4:13
"I can do everything through him who gives me strength."

Isaiah 53:5
"But he was pierced for our transgressions, he was crushed for our iniquities; the punishment that brought us peace was upon him, and by his wounds we are healed."

Matthew 8:17
"................"He took up our infirmities and carried our diseases."

John 8:36
"So if the Son sets you free, you will be free indeed."

Romans 8:32
"He who did not spare his own Son, but gave him up for us all-how will he not also, along with him, graciously give us all things?"

Colossians 1:13
"For he has rescued us from the dominion of darkness and brought us into the kingdom of the Son he loves"

Isaiah 51:16
"I have put my words in your mouth and covered you with the shadow of my hand"

Isaiah 43:18
"Forget the former things; do not dwell on the past.

Hebrews 2:14-15
"Since the children have flesh and blood, he too shared in their humanity so that by his death he might destroy him who holds the power of death-that is, the devil- 15and free those who all their lives were held in slavery by their fear of death."

1 John 5:4-5
4 "for everyone born of God overcomes the world. This is the victory that has overcome the world, even our faith. 5Who is it that overcomes the world? Only he who believes that Jesus is the Son of God.

Chapter 23

Marriage

There is a life partner ordained for everyone. No one excluded. Claim yours in prayer through the words of God. Sow seeds of God words into your marriage and into your troubled marriages. the power in the word can change things and situations.

> **Instructions:** All scriptures are taken from New International Version (NIV) Start reading every scripture out aloud with: **"It is written......"**
>
> **SAMPLE VERSE:** - "The hands of Zerubbabel have laid the foundation of this temple; his hands will also complete it...."
> **Read Like This**
> It is written - "The hands of **(Your Name)** have laid the foundation of this temple; **(My)** hands will also complete it.... "

It is written..... Genesis 2:24
"For this reason a man will leave his father and mother and be united to his wife, and they will become one flesh."

Genesis 2:23
"The man said, "This is now bone of my bones and flesh of my flesh; she shall be called 'woman, 'for she was taken out of man."

Genesis 2:25
" The man and his wife were both naked, and they felt no shame. "

Isaiah 34:16
" Look in the scroll of the LORD and read: None of these will be missing, not one will lack her mate. For it is his mouth that has given the order, and his Spirit will gather them together."

Matthew 19:6
"So they are no longer two, but one. Therefore what God has joined together, let man not separate."

2 Corinthians 12:9
"But he said to me, "My grace is sufficient for you, for my power is made perfect in weakness." Therefore I will boast all the more gladly about my weaknesses, so that Christ's power may rest on me. "

Malachi 2:14
"............ the LORD hath been witness between thee and the wife of thy youth, against whom thou hast dealt treacherously: yet is she thy companion, and the wife of thy covenant."

Malachi 2:15
"And did not he make one? Yet had he the residue of the spirit. And wherefore one? That he might seek a godly seed. Therefore take heed to your spirit, and let none deal treacherously against the wife of his youth."

1 Corinthians 7:2
"...... to avoid fornication, let every man have his own wife, and let every woman have her own husband."

1 Corinthians 7:3
"Let the husband render unto the wife due benevolence: and likewise also the wife unto the husband."

1 Corinthians 7:4
"The wife hath not power of her own body, but the husband: and likewise also the husband hath not power of his own body, but the wife."

1 Corinthians 7:10
"And unto the married I command, yet not I, but the Lord, Let not the wife depart from her husband:"

1 Corinthians 7:12
"But to the rest speak I, not the Lord: If any brother hath a wife that believeth not, and she be pleased to dwell with him, let him not put her away."

1 Corinthians 7:14
"For the unbelieving husband is sanctified by the wife, and the unbelieving wife is sanctified by the husband: else were your children unclean; but now are they holy."

1 Corinthians 7:27
"Art thou bound unto a wife? seek not to be loosed. Art thou loosed from a wife? seek not a wife."

Chapter 24

Overwhelmed

This is a devise and strategy of the enemy to get you to lose your focus on God. Speak the word and defend your self establishing your life a no touch area. Nothing is to great that God has not already finished in your life.

> **Instructions:** All scriptures are taken from New International Version (NIV) Start reading every scripture out aloud with: ***"It is written......"***
>
> **SAMPLE VERSE:** - "The hands of Zerubbabel have laid the foundation of this temple; his hands will also complete it...."
> **Read Like This**
> **It is written** - "The hands of *(Your Name)* have laid the foundation of this temple; *(My)* hands will also complete it.... "

It is written..... Psalm 68:1
"May God arise, may his enemies be scattered; may his foes flee before him."

Psalm 18:29
"With your help I can advance against a troop ; with my God I can scale a wall."

Psalm 20:7
"Some trust in chariots and some in horses, but we trust in the name of the LORD our God."

1 Samuel 15:29
"He who is the Glory of Israel does not lie or change his mind; for he is not a man, that he should change his mind."

Psalm 23:2
"He makes me lie down in green pastures, he leads me beside quiet waters"

Judges 6:14
"................ "Go in the strength you have and save Israel out of Midian's hand. Am I not sending you?"

Isaiah 12:2
"Surely God is my salvation; I will trust and not be afraid. The LORD, the LORD, is my strength and my song; he has become my salvation."

Isaiah 30:15
" This is what the Sovereign LORD, the Holy One of Israel, says: "In repentance and rest is your salvation, in quietness and trust is your strength, ..."

Isaiah 40:31
"but those who hope in the LORD will renew their strength. They will soar on wings like eagles;
they will run and not grow weary,
they will walk and not be faint."

Isaiah 43:2
"When you pass through the waters, I will be with you; and when you pass through the rivers, they will not sweep over you. When you walk through the fire, you will not be burned; the flames will not set you ablaze."

2 Corinthians 12:9
"But he said to me, "My grace is sufficient for you, for my power is made perfect in weakness." Therefore I will boast all the more gladly about my weaknesses, so that Christ's power may rest on me."

2 Corinthians 12:10
"That is why, for Christ's sake, I delight in weaknesses, in insults, in hardships, in persecutions, in difficulties. For when I am weak, then I am strong."

Psalm 2:8
"Ask of me, and I will make the nations your inheritance, the ends of the earth your possession."

Psalm 1:5-6
5 "Therefore the wicked will not stand in the judgment, nor sinners in the assembly of the righteous.
6 For the LORD watches over the way of the righteous, but the way of the wicked will perish."

Psalm 24:1
"The earth is the LORD's, and everything in it, the world, and all who live in it"

Proverbs 10:27-28
27 The fear of the LORD adds length to life, but the years of the wicked are cut short.
28 The prospect of the righteous is joy, but the hopes of the wicked come to nothing."

Psalm 55:22
"Cast your cares on the LORD and he will sustain you; he will never let the righteous fall.......But as for me, I trust in you."

Proverbs 9:11
"For through me your days will be many, and years will be added to your life."

Psalm 50:15
" and call upon me in the day of trouble; I will deliver you, and you will honor me."

Psalm 20:6
"Now I know that the LORD saves his anointed; he answers him from his holy heaven with the saving power of his right hand."

Psalm 18:23
"I have been blameless before him and have kept myself from sin."

Psalm 18:48-49
[48] "who saves me from my enemies. You exalted me above my foes; from violent men you rescued me. [49] Therefore I will praise you among the nations, O LORD; I will sing praises to your name.

Psalm 16:8
" I have set the LORD always before me. Because he is at my right hand, I will not be shaken."

Chapter 25

Peace Of God

When the enemy is out to destroy your peace, speak the words of God that will grab hold of your peace re-establishing it back into your life.

> **Instructions:** All scriptures are taken from New International Version (NIV) Start reading every scripture out aloud with: ***"It is written......"***
>
> **SAMPLE VERSE:** - "The hands of Zerubbabel have laid the foundation of this temple; his hands will also complete it...."
> **Read Like This**
> **It is written** - "The hands of *(Your Name)* have laid the foundation of this temple; *(My)* hands will also complete it.... "

It is written..... Leviticus 26:6
" 'I will grant peace in the land, and you will lie down and no one will make you afraid. I will remove savage beasts from the land, and the sword will not pass through your country."

John 14:27
"Peace I leave with you; my peace I give you. I do not give to you as the world gives. Do not let your hearts be troubled and do not be afraid."

Job 22:21
"Submit to God and be at peace with him; in this way prosperity will come to you."

Psalm 4:8
"I will lie down and sleep in peace, for you alone, O LORD, make me dwell in safety."

Psalm 29:11
"The LORD gives strength to his people; the LORD blesses his people with peace."

Psalm 34:14
"Depart from evil, and do good; seek peace, and pursue it."

Psalm 37:37
"Consider the blameless, observe the upright; there is a future for the man of peace."

Psalm 55:18
"He hath delivered my soul in peace from the battle that was against me: for there were many with me."

Psalm 122:7
"Peace be within thy walls, and prosperity within thy palaces."

Psalm 147:14
"He grants peace to your borders and satisfies you with the finest of wheat."

Psalm 37:11
"But the meek will inherit the land and enjoy great peace."

Proverbs 14:30
"A heart at peace gives life to the body, but envy rots the bones."

Proverbs 16:7
"When a man's ways are pleasing to the LORD, he makes even his enemies live at peace with him."

Proverbs 11:12
"A man who lacks judgment derides his neighbor, but a man of understanding holds his tongue."

Isaiah 26:3
"You will keep in perfect peace him whose mind is steadfast, because he trusts in you."

Isaiah 27:5
"Or let him take hold of my strength, that he may make peace with me; and he shall make peace with me."

Isaiah 32:17
"And the work of righteousness shall be peace; and the effect of righteousness quietness
and assurance for ever."

Isaiah 32:18
"And my people shall dwell in a peaceable habitation, and in sure dwellings, and in quiet resting places;"

Psalm 37:37
"Consider the blameless, observe the upright; there is a future for the man of peace"

Isaiah 54:10
"Though the mountains be shaken and the hills be removed, yet my unfailing love for you will not be shaken nor my covenant of peace be removed," says the LORD, who has compassion on you."

Isaiah 55:12
"For ye shall go out with joy, and be led forth with peace: the mountains and the hills shall break forth before you into singing, and all the trees of the field shall clap their hands."

2 Samuel 23:5
"Is not my house right with God? Has he not made with me an everlasting covenant, arranged and secured in every part? Will he not bring to fruition my salvation and grant me my every desire?"

Psalm 127:1
"Unless the LORD builds the house, its builders labor in vain. Unless the LORD watches over the city, the watchmen stand guard in vain."

Chapter 26

Prosperity - Divine Health

This is different from divine healing. This is a making a demand for a state of permanent wellness. Never sick! What you say you are through the word of God is what you will be!

> **Instructions:** All scriptures are taken from New International Version (NIV) Start reading every scripture out aloud with: ***"It is written......"***
>
> **SAMPLE VERSE:** - "The hands of Zerubbabel have laid the foundation of this temple; his hands will also complete it...."
> **Read Like This**
> **It is written** - "The hands of *(Your Name)* have laid the foundation of this temple; *(My)* hands will also complete it.... "

*It is written..... * **Psalm 52:8**
"But I am like an olive tree flourishing in the house of God; I trust in God's unfailing love for ever and ever."

Psalm 91:16
"With long life will I satisfy him and show him my salvation."

Psalm 34:20
"He protects all his bones, not one of them will be broken"

Job 5:26
"You will come to the grave in full vigor, like sheaves gathered in season."

Jeremiah 30:17
"But I will restore you to health and heal your wounds,' 'because you are called an outcast, Zion for whom no one cares."

Hebrews 12:12
"Therefore, strengthen your feeble arms and weak knees."

2 Peter 1:3
"His divine power has given us everything we need for life and godliness through our knowledge of him who called us by his own glory and goodness."

1 Samuel 25:6
"......... 'Long life to you! Good health to you and your household! And good health to all that is yours!"

Psalm 73:4
"They have no struggles; their bodies are healthy and strong."

Proverbs 3:7- 8
7"Do not be wise in your own eyes; fear the LORD and shun evil. 8 This will bring health to your body and nourishment to your bones.

Jeremiah 30:17
"But I will restore you to health and heal your wounds,' declares the LORD, 'because you are called an outcast, Zion for whom no one cares."

Jeremiah 33:6
".......I will bring health and healing to it; I will heal my people and will let them enjoy abundant peace and security."

Proverbs 10:12
"Hatred stirs up dissension, but love covers over all wrongs."

Proverbs 9:11
"For through me your days will be many, and years will be added to your life."

3 John 1:2
"........ you may enjoy good health and that all may go well with you, even as your soul is getting along well."

Chapter 27

Prosperity - Wealth

This is a permanent place of riches and wealth. Not the 9-5 kind of riches, but the kind of wealth that God can give you: above and beyond your imagination! Claim it and believe what you say.

Instructions: All scriptures are taken from New International Version (NIV) Start reading every scripture out aloud with: *"It is written......"*

SAMPLE VERSE: - "The hands of Zerubbabel have laid the foundation of this temple; his hands will also complete it...."
Read Like This
It is written - "The hands of *(Your Name)* have laid the foundation of this temple; *(My)* hands will also complete it.... "

It is written..... Micah 7:11
"The day for building your walls will come, the day for extending your boundaries."

Psalm 147:14
"He grants peace to your borders and satisfies you with the finest of wheat."

Isaiah 60:18
"No longer will violence be heard in your land, nor ruin or destruction within your borders, but you will call your walls Salvation and your gates Praise."

Isaiah 54:12
"And I will make thy windows of agates, and thy gates of carbuncles, and all thy borders of pleasant stones."

Psalm 16:6
"The boundary lines have fallen for me in pleasant places; surely I have a delightful inheritance."

Isaiah 60:10
"Foreigners will rebuild your walls, and their kings will serve you. Though in anger I struck you, in favor I will show you compassion."

Isaiah 62:8
"The LORD has sworn by his right hand and by his mighty arm: "Never again will I give your grain as food for your enemies, and never again will foreigners drink the new wine for which you have toiled"

Leviticus 20:24
"............, "You will possess their land; I will give it to you as an inheritance, a land flowing with milk and honey." I am the LORD your God, who has set you apart from the nations."

1 Chronicles 16:18
"To you I will give the land of Canaan as the portion you will inherit."

Psalm 16:5
5 "LORD, you have assigned me my portion and my cup; you have made my lot secure. The boundary lines have fallen for me in pleasant places; surely I have a delightful inheritance.

Psalm 25:13
"He will spend his days in prosperity, and his descendants will inherit the land."

Psalm 37:11
"But the meek will inherit the land and enjoy great peace"

Psalm 23:5-6
5 "You prepare a table before me in the presence of my enemies. You anoint my head with oil; my cup overflows. 6 Surely goodness and love will follow me all the days of my life, and I will dwell in the house of the LORD forever.

Psalm 37:29
"the righteous will inherit the land and dwell in it forever."

Psalm 68:9
"You gave abundant showers, O God; you refreshed your weary inheritance."

Daniel 11:32
"…………..: but the people that do know their God shall be strong, and do exploits."

Matthew 5:5
"Blessed are the meek, for they will inherit the earth."

Job 5:23
"For you will have a covenant with the stones of the field, and the wild animals will be at peace with you."

Numbers 14:8
"If the LORD is pleased with us, he will lead us into that land, a land flowing with milk and honey, and will give it to us."

Numbers 23:21
"No misfortune is seen in Jacob, no misery observed in Israel. The LORD their God is with them; the shout of the King is among them."

Joshua 1:3
"I will give you every place where you set your foot, as I promised Moses"

Matthew 18:19
"................... if two of you on earth agree about anything you ask for, it will be done for you by my Father in heaven."

2 Corinthians 9:10
"Now he who supplies seed to the sower and bread for food will also supply and increase your store of seed and will enlarge the harvest of your righteousness."

Isaiah 54:2-3

2 "Enlarge the place of your tent, stretch your tent curtains wide, do not hold back; lengthen your cords, strengthen your stakes. 3 For you will spread out to the right and to the left; your descendants will dispossess nations and settle in their desolate cities.

Matthew 17:20

"........................ I tell you the truth, if you have faith as small as a mustard seed, you can say to this mountain, 'Move from here to there' and it will move. Nothing will be impossible for you."

2 Peter 3:9

"The Lord is not slow in keeping his promise, as some understand slowness."

Revelation 3:8

8I know your deeds. See, I have placed before you an open door that no one can shut. I know that you have little strength, yet you have kept my word and have not denied my name.

Deuteronomy 11:15

"I will provide grass in the fields for your cattle, and you will eat and be satisfied."

2 Samuel 7:10

"And I will provide a place for my people Israel and will plant them so that they can have a home of their own and no longer be disturbed. Wicked people will not oppress them anymore, as they did at the beginning"

Zechariah 8:13
" As you have been an object of cursing among the nations, O Judah and Israel, so will I save you, and you will be a blessing. Do not be afraid, but let your hands be strong."

Deuteronomy 8:18
18 But remember the LORD your God, for it is he who gives you the ability to produce wealth, and so confirms his covenant, which he swore to your forefathers, as it is today.

Hosea 2:8
"She has not acknowledged that I was the one who gave her the grain, the new wine and oil, who lavished on her the silver and gold; which they used for Baal"

Exodus 23:25
"Worship the LORD your God, and his blessing will be on your food and water. I will take away sickness from among you"

Exodus 19:5
"Now if you obey me fully and keep my covenant, then out of all nations you will be my treasured possession. Although the whole earth is mine"

Chapter 28

Purpose - On Earth
(Pre-ordination)

Use this scriptures to talk to God; He will show you what your purpose is, or He will establish your calling in Him according to your declaration.

> **Instructions:** All scriptures are taken from New International Version (NIV) Start reading every scripture out aloud with: ***"It is written......"***
>
> **SAMPLE VERSE:** - "The hands of Zerubbabel have laid the foundation of this temple; his hands will also complete it...."
> **Read Like This**
> It is written - "The hands of *(Your Name)* have laid the foundation of this temple; *(My)* hands will also complete it.... "

It is written..... Psalm 138:8
"The LORD will fulfill his purpose for me; your love, O LORD, endures forever; do not abandon the works of your hands."

Isaiah 14:24
"The LORD Almighty has sworn, "Surely, as I have planned, so it will be, and as I have purposed, so it will stand."

Isaiah 14:27
"For the LORD Almighty has purposed, and who can thwart him? His hand is stretched out, and who can turn it back?"

Isaiah 42:6-7

⁶ "I, the LORD, have called you in righteousness; I will take hold of your hand. I will keep you and will make you to be a covenant for the people and a light for the Gentiles, ⁷ to open eyes that are blind, to free captives from prison and to release from the dungeon those who sit in darkness

Isaiah 51:16

" I have put my words in your mouth and covered you with the shadow of my hand- I who set the heavens in place, who laid the foundations of the earth, and who say to Zion, 'You are my people. "

Jeremiah 15:11

"The LORD said, "Surely I will deliver you for a good purpose; surely I will make your enemies plead with you in times of disaster and times of distress."

Zechariah 8:13

"As you have been an object of cursing among the nations, O Judah and Israel, so will I save you, and you will be a blessing. Do not be afraid, but let your hands be strong."

Luke 9:62

"........ "No one who puts his hand to the plow and looks back is fit for service in the kingdom of God."

2 Corinthians 3:17

"Now the Lord is the Spirit, and where the Spirit of the Lord is, there is freedom."

Matthew 17:20
"He replied, "Because you have so little faith. I tell you the truth, if you have faith as small as a mustard seed, you can say to this mountain, 'Move from here to there' and it will move. Nothing will be impossible for you."

2 Corinthians 9:10
"Now he who supplies seed to the sower and bread for food will also supply and increase your store of seed and will enlarge the harvest of your righteousness."

Ephesians 3:20
"Now to him who is able to do immeasurably more than all we ask or imagine, according to his power that is at work within us"

Revelation 3:8
"I know your deeds. See, I have placed before you an open door that no one can shut. I know that you have little strength, yet you have kept my word and have not denied my name."

John 14:12
"I tell you the truth, anyone who has faith in me will do what I have been doing. He will do even greater things than these, because I am going to the Father."

IT IS WRITTEN ... (YOUR SPIRITUAL SWORD & SHIELD)

Chapter 29

Purpose - Ministry

This is for those who have identified that they have a calling in God in the spiritual things. Speak the words to establish power, provision and dominion in Ministry.

> **Instructions:** All scriptures are taken from New International Version (NIV) Start reading every scripture out aloud with: ***"It is written......"***
>
> **SAMPLE VERSE:** - "The hands of Zerubbabel have laid the foundation of this temple; his hands will also complete it...."
> **Read Like This**
> **It is written** - "The hands of *(Your Name)* have laid the foundation of this temple; *(My)* hands will also complete it.... "

It is written..... Isaiah 52:7
"How beautiful on the mountains are the feet of those who bring good news, who proclaim peace, who bring good tidings, who proclaim salvation, who say to Zion, "Your God reigns!"

Isaiah 59:21
"As for me, this is my covenant with them," says the LORD. "My Spirit, who is on you, and my words that I have put in your mouth will not depart from your mouth, or from the mouths of your children, or from the mouths of their descendants from this time on and forever," says the LORD."

Isaiah 61:1
"The Spirit of the Sovereign LORD is on me, because the LORD has anointed me to preach good news to the poor. He has sent me to bind up the brokenhearted, to proclaim freedom for the captives and release from darkness for the prisoners"

2 Corinthians 9:10
"Now he who supplies seed to the sower and bread for food will also supply and increase your store of seed and will enlarge the harvest of your righteousness."

2 Timothy 4:5
"But you, keep your head in all situations, endure hardship, do the work of an evangelist, discharge all the duties of your ministry."

Revelation 3:8
"I know your deeds. See, I have placed before you an open door that no one can shut. I know that you have little strength, yet you have kept my word and have not denied my name."

John 14:12
"I tell you the truth, anyone who has faith in me will do what I have been doing. He will do even greater things than these, because I am going to the Father."

1 Corinthians 12:31
"But eagerly desire the greater gifts. And now I will show you the most excellent way."

1 John 4:4
"You, dear children, are from God and have overcome them, because the one who is in you is greater than the one who is in the world."

Acts 20:28
28Keep watch over yourselves and all the flock of which the Holy Spirit has made you overseers. Be shepherds of the church of God, which he bought with his own blood.

Ephesians 1:18
"I pray also that the eyes of your heart may be enlightened in order that you may know the hope to which he has called you, the riches of his glorious inheritance in the saints"

1 Corinthians 7:23
"You were bought at a price; do not become slaves of men. 24Brothers, each man, as responsible to God, should remain in the situation God called him to."

Romans 8:30
30And those he predestined, he also called; those he called, he also justified; those he justified, he also glorified.

1 Corinthians 12:7
"Now to each one the manifestation of the Spirit is given for the common good.

John 14:10-14

"I tell you the truth, anyone who has faith in me will do what I have been doing. He will do even greater things than these, because I am going to the Father."

Chapter 30

Resisting The Devil

This is a chapter to be read in just about every situation of attack in life. These scriptures speak to you to encourage you; to rebuke the enemy; and to stand on the promises of God.

> **Instructions:** All scriptures are taken from New International Version (NIV) Start reading every scripture out aloud with: ***"It is written......"***
>
> **SAMPLE VERSE:** - "The hands of Zerubbabel have laid the foundation of this temple; his hands will also complete it...."
> **Read Like This**
> **It is written** - "The hands of *(Your Name)* have laid the foundation of this temple; *(My)* hands will also complete it.... "

It is written..... 1 Peter 5:9
"Resist him, standing firm in the faith, because you know that your brothers throughout the world are undergoing the same kind of sufferings."

James 4:7
"Submit yourselves, then, to God. Resist the devil, and he will flee from you."

Daniel 11:32
"With flattery he will corrupt those who have violated the covenant, but the people who know their God will firmly resist him"

Isaiah 49:25
" .... the LORD says: "Yes, captives will be taken from warriors, and plunder retrieved from the fierce; I will contend with those who contend with you, and your children I will save."

Zechariah 2:5
"And I myself will be a wall of fire around it,' declares the LORD, 'and I will be its glory within."

Zechariah 4:6
" So he said to me, "This is the word of the LORD to Zerubbabel: 'Not by might nor by power, but by my Spirit,' says the LORD Almighty."

Zechariah 4:9
"The hands of Zerubbabel have laid the foundation of this temple; his hands will also complete it. Then you will know that the LORD Almighty has sent me to you."

Galatians 6:17
".......... let no one cause me trouble, for I bear on my body the marks of Jesus."

Philippians 2:10
"that at the name of Jesus every knee should bow, in heaven and on earth and under the earth"

Hebrews 12:29
"for our "God is a consuming fire."

2 Timothy 4:5
"But you, keep your head in all situations"

1 Peter 5:8
"Be self-controlled and alert. Your enemy the devil prowls around like a roaring lion looking for someone to devour."

Jude 1:9
"........., "The Lord rebuke you!"

Revelation 12:11
"They overcame him by the blood of the Lamb and by the word of their testimony; they did not love their lives so much as to shrink from death."

1 John 3:8
".......The reason the Son of God appeared was to destroy the devil's work."

Colossians 2:15
"And having disarmed the powers and authorities, he made a public spectacle of them, triumphing over them by the cross.

Luke 10:19
"I have given you authority to trample on snakes and scorpions and to overcome all the power of the enemy; nothing will harm you.

Luke 9:1
"................... he gave them power and authority to drive out all demons and to cure diseases

Psalm 18:44
"As soon as they hear me, they obey me; foreigners cringe before me."

Job 5:12-13
12 He thwarts the plans of the crafty, so that their hands achieve no success. 13 He catches the wise in their craftiness, and the schemes of the wily are swept away.

Hebrews 2:8
"and put everything under his feet." In putting everything under him, God left nothing that is not subject to him. Yet at present we do not see everything subject to him.

Psalm 24:1
"The earth is the LORD's, and everything in it, the world, and all who live in it"

Mark 16:17-18
17 And these signs will accompany those who believe: In my name they will drive out demons; they will speak in new tongues; 18 they will pick up snakes with their hands; and when they drink deadly poison, it will not hurt them at all; they will place their hands on sick people, and they will get well."

Chapter 31

Resisting Temptation

Resisting temptation is you trying to take control of your ungodly and sinful desires. The enemy may bring the temptation but falling into it, is your choice.

> **Instructions:** All scriptures are taken from New International Version (NIV) Start reading every scripture out aloud with: ***"It is written......"***
>
> **SAMPLE VERSE:** - "The hands of Zerubbabel have laid the foundation of this temple; his hands will also complete it...."
> **Read Like This**
> It is written - "The hands of *(Your Name)* have laid the foundation of this temple; *(My)* hands will also complete it.... "

It is written..... Matthew 6:13
"And lead us not into temptation, but deliver us from the evil one."

1 Corinthians 7:5
"Do not deprive each other except by mutual consent and for a time, so that you may devote yourselves to prayer. Then come together again so that Satan will not tempt you because of your lack of self-control."

Galatians 6:1
"Brothers, if someone is caught in a sin, you who are spiritual should restore him gently. But watch yourself, or you also may be tempted."

1 Corinthians 10:13
"No temptation has seized you except what is common to man. And God is faithful; he will not let you be tempted beyond what you can bear. But when you are tempted, he will also provide a way out so that you can stand up under it"

Hebrews 2:18
"Because he himself suffered when he was tempted, he is able to help those who are being tempted."

Hebrews 3:8
"do not harden your hearts as you did in the rebellion, during the time of testing in the desert"

James 1:12
"Blessed is the man who perseveres under trial, because when he has stood the test, he will receive the crown of life that God has promised to those who love him."

2 Peter 2:9
"if this is so, then the Lord knows how to rescue godly men from trials and to hold the unrighteous for the day of judgment, while continuing their punishment."

Matthew 5:39
"But I tell you, Do not resist an evil person. If someone strikes you on the right cheek, turn to him the other also"

Hebrews 12:4
"In your struggle against sin, you have not yet resisted to the point of shedding your blood."

James 4:6
"But he gives us more grace. That is why Scripture says: "God opposes the proud but gives grace to the humble."

James 4:7
"Submit yourselves, then, to God. Resist the devil, and he will flee from you."

1 Peter 5:9
"Resist him, standing firm in the faith, because you know that your brothers throughout the world are undergoing the same kind of sufferings."

Job 5:12-13
12 "He thwarts the plans of the crafty,
so that their hands achieve no success.
13 He catches the wise in their craftiness,
and the schemes of the wily are swept away."

Jeremiah 4:15
"A voice is announcing from Dan,
proclaiming disaster from the hills of Ephraim."

IT IS WRITTEN ... (YOUR SPIRITUAL SWORD & SHIELD)

Chapter 32

Restoration

After many years of affliction, a lot of damage will be done to the body, even after deliverance and healing. The body will need to be restored, especially through the words of God in prayer!

Instructions: All scriptures are taken from New International Version (NIV) Start reading every scripture out aloud with: **"It is written......"**

SAMPLE VERSE: - "The hands of Zerubbabel have laid the foundation of this temple; his hands will also complete it...."
Read Like This
It is written - "The hands of *(Your Name)* have laid the foundation of this temple; *(My)* hands will also complete it.... "

It is written...Isaiah 57:18
"I have seen his ways, but I will heal him; I will guide him and restore comfort to him"

Jeremiah 30:17
"But I will restore you to health and heal your wounds,' declares the LORD, 'because you are called an outcast, Zion for whom no one cares."

Jeremiah 31:18
"I have surely heard Ephraim's moaning: 'You disciplined me like an unruly calf, and I have been disciplined. Restore me, and I will return, because you are the LORD my God."

Zephaniah 3:20
"At that time I will gather you; at that time I will bring you home. I will give you honor and praise among all the peoples of the earth when I restore your fortunes before your very eyes," says the LORD."

Zechariah 9:12
"Return to your fortress, O prisoners of hope; even now I announce that I will restore twice as much to you."

Psalm 71:20-21
20 "Though you have made me see troubles, many and bitter, you will restore my life again; from the depths of the earth you will again bring me up.
21 You will increase my honor and comfort me once again."

Isaiah 41:12-13
12 Though you search for your enemies, you will not find them. Those who wage war against you will be as nothing at all.
13 For I am the LORD, your God, who takes hold of your right hand and says to you, Do not fear; I will help you.

Isaiah 43:1
"But now, this is what the LORD says; he who created you, O Jacob, he who formed you, O Israel: "Fear not, for I have redeemed you; I have summoned you by name; you are mine."

Isaiah 60:10
"Foreigners will rebuild your walls, and their kings will serve you. Though in anger I struck you, in favor I will show you compassion.

Isaiah 60:15
"Although you have been forsaken and hated, with no one traveling through, I will make you the everlasting pride and the joy of all generations."

Isaiah 61:7
"Instead of their shame my people will receive a double portion, and instead of disgrace they will rejoice in their inheritance; and so they will inherit a double portion in their land, and everlasting joy will be theirs."

Jeremiah 31:4
"I will build you up again and you will be rebuilt, O Virgin Israel. Again you will take up your tambourines and go out to dance with the joyful."

Ezekiel 37:13
"Then you, my people, will know that I am the LORD, when I open your graves and bring you up from them."

Zechariah 9:12
"Return to your fortress, O prisoners of hope; even now I announce that I will restore twice as much to you."

Matthew 21:22
"If you believe, you will receive whatever you ask for in prayer."

Matthew 21:21

"Jesus replied, "I tell you the truth, if you have faith and do not doubt, not only can you do what was done to the fig tree, but also you can say to this mountain, 'Go, throw yourself into the sea,' and it will be done."

2 Peter 3:9

"The Lord is not slow in keeping his promise, as some understand slowness. He is patient with you, not wanting anyone to perish, but everyone to come to repentance."

Chapter 33

Safety In Trouble

In the times of present trouble, there is help through the words of God. These are words to be memorized, so that they flow through your spirit when you need them. A present help in time of need.

> **Instructions:** All scriptures are taken from New International Version (NIV) Start reading every scripture out aloud with: ***"It is written......"***
>
> **SAMPLE VERSE:** - "The hands of Zerubbabel have laid the foundation of this temple; his hands will also complete it...."
> **Read Like This**
> It is written - "The hands of *(Your Name)* have laid the foundation of this temple; *(My)* hands will also complete it.... "

It is written..... Psalm 27:5
" For in the day of trouble he will keep me safe in his dwelling; he will hide me in the shelter of his tabernacle and set me high upon a rock."

Psalm 10:12
" Arise, LORD! Lift up your hand, O God. Do not forget the helpless."

Psalm 18:19
"He brought me out into a spacious place; he rescued me because he delighted in me."

Galatians 6:17
"Finally, let no one cause me trouble, for I bear on my body the marks of Jesus."

Psalm 28:7
"The LORD is my strength and my shield; my heart trusts in him, and I am helped. My heart leaps for joy and I will give thanks to him in song."

Psalm 9:9
"The LORD is a refuge for the oppressed, a stronghold in times of trouble."

Numbers 23:19
"God is not a man, that he should lie, nor a son of man, that he should change his mind. Does he speak and then not act? Does he promise and not fulfill?"

Galatians 5:10
"I am confident in the Lord that you will take no other view. The one who is throwing you into confusion will pay the penalty, whoever he may be."

Psalm 138:7
"Though I walk in the midst of trouble, you preserve my life; you stretch out your hand against the anger of my foes, with your right hand you save me. "

Jeremiah 23:23
"Am I only a God nearby," declares the LORD, "and not a God far away?"

Psalm 23:4
"Even though I walk through the valley of the shadow of death, I will fear no evil, for you are with me; your rod and your staff, they comfort me.

Psalm 27:11
Teach me your way, O LORD; lead me in a straight path because of my oppressors.

Isaiah 43:2
2 When you pass through the waters, I will be with you; and when you pass through the rivers, they will not sweep over you. When you walk through the fire, you will not be burned; the flames will not set you ablaze.

Jeremiah 20:11
" But the LORD is with me like a mighty warrior; so my persecutors will stumble and not prevail. They will fail and be thoroughly disgraced; their dishonor will never be forgotten.

Psalm 9:9-10
9"The LORD is a refuge for the oppressed, a stronghold in times of trouble. 10 Those who know your name will trust in you, for you, LORD, have never forsaken those who seek you.

Psalm 9:3
My enemies turn back; they stumble and perish before you.

Psalm 4:8
"I will lie down and sleep in peace,
for you alone, O LORD, make me dwell in safety."

Psalm 5:11-12
¹¹ But let all who take refuge in you be glad; let them ever sing for joy. Spread your protection over them, that those who love your name may rejoice in you. ¹² For surely, O LORD, you bless the righteous; you surround them with your favor as with a shield.

Psalm 1:1
"Blessed is the man who does not walk in the counsel of the wicked or stand in the way of sinners or sit in the seat of mockers."

Psalm 3:3
"But you are a shield around me, O LORD; you bestow glory on me and lift up my head."

Psalm 105:15
"Do not touch my anointed ones; do my prophets no harm."

Chapter 34

Security

Secure your life through the word of God. Speak the words to yourself to give your spirit an assurance that God has got your secured and preserved. No harm will come to you!

> **Instructions:** All scriptures are taken from New International Version (NIV) Start reading every scripture out aloud with: ***"It is written......"***
>
> **SAMPLE VERSE:** - "The hands of Zerubbabel have laid the foundation of this temple; his hands will also complete it...."
> **Read Like This**
> It is written - "The hands of *(Your Name)* have laid the foundation of this temple; *(My)* hands will also complete it.... "

It is written..... Psalm 18:36
"You broaden the path beneath me, so that my ankles do not turn."

Job 5:24
"You will know that your tent is secure; you will take stock of your property and find nothing missing."

2 Samuel 23:5
"Is not my house right with God? Has he not made with me an everlasting covenant, arranged and secured in every part? Will he not bring to fruition my salvation and grant me my every desire?"

Genesis 28:15
"I am with you and will watch over you wherever you go, and I will bring you back to this land. I will not leave you until I have done what I have promised you."

Psalm 27:2
" When evil men advance against me to devour my flesh, when my enemies and my foes attack me, they will stumble and fall."

Isaiah 54:14
"In righteousness you will be established: Tyranny will be far from you; you will have nothing to fear. Terror will be far removed; it will not come near you."

Isaiah 65:24
"Before they call I will answer; while they are still speaking I will hear."

Matthew 18:18
"I tell you the truth, whatever you bind on earth will be bound in heaven, and whatever you loose on earth will be loosed in heaven."

Matthew 21:22
"If you believe, you will receive whatever you ask for in prayer."

Leviticus 25:19
"Then the land will yield its fruit, and you will eat your fill and live there in safety"

Leviticus 26:5
"Your threshing will continue until grape harvest and the grape harvest will continue until planting, and you will eat all the food you want
and live in safety in your land

Psalm 27:5
For in the day of trouble he will keep me safe in his dwelling; he will hide me in the shelter of his tabernacle and set me high upon a rock.

Psalm 78:53
He guided them safely, so they were unafraid; but the sea engulfed their enemies.

Proverbs 3:23
Then you will go on your way in safety, and your foot will not stumble;

1 John 5:18
We know that anyone born of God does not continue to sin; the one who was born of God keeps him safe, and the evil one cannot harm him.

IT IS WRITTEN ... (YOUR SPIRITUAL SWORD & SHIELD)

Chapter 35

Seeking Information from God

The word of God says that, we can ask God anything, if we believe that He will answer, you will get a reply. The scriptures to establish your demand for information is below.

> **Instructions:** All scriptures are taken from New International Version (NIV) Start reading every scripture out aloud with: **"It is written......"**
>
> **SAMPLE VERSE:** - "The hands of Zerubbabel have laid the foundation of this temple; his hands will also complete it...."
> **Read Like This**
> It is written - "The hands of *(Your Name)* have laid the foundation of this temple; *(My)* hands will also complete it.... "

It is written..... Psalm 27:4
One thing I ask of the LORD, this is what I seek: that I may dwell in the house of the LORD all the days of my life, to gaze upon the beauty of the LORD and to seek him in his temple

Psalm 34:10
The lions may grow weak and hungry, but those who seek the LORD lack no good thing

Psalm 27:8
My heart says of you, "Seek his face!" Your face, LORD, I will seek.

Jeremiah 33:2-3

2 "This is what the LORD says, he who made the earth, the LORD who formed it and established it—the LORD is his name: 3 'Call to me and I will answer you and tell you great and unsearchable things you do not know.'

Proverbs 20:18

"Make plans by seeking advice; if you wage war, obtain guidance."

Isaiah 45:19

"I have not spoken in secret, from somewhere in a land of darkness; I have not said to Jacob's descendants, 'Seek me in vain.' I, the LORD, speak the truth; I declare what is right."

Isaiah 51:1

"Listen to me, you who pursue righteousness and who seek the LORD : Look to the rock from which you were cut and to the quarry from which you were hewn;"

Isaiah 55:6

"Seek the LORD while he may be found; call on him while he is near."

Jeremiah 29:13

"You will seek me and find me when you seek me with all your heart."

Matthew 6:33

"But seek first his kingdom and his righteousness, and all these things will be given to you as well."

Matthew 7:7
"Ask and it will be given to you;
seek and you will find; knock and the door will be opened to you."

Matthew 7:8
"For everyone who asks receives; he who
seeks finds; and to him who knocks,
the door will be opened."

Luke 11:10
"For everyone who asks receives; he who
seeks finds; and to him who knocks,
the door will be opened."

Acts 17:27
"God did this so that men would seek
him and perhaps reach out for him and find him,
though he is not far from each one of us"

Isaiah 65:24
"Before they call I will answer; while they are still
speaking I will hear."

2 Peter 3:9
"The Lord is not slow in keeping his promise, as some
understand slowness. He is patient with you,
not wanting anyone to perish,
but everyone
to come to repentance."

Daniel 2:28
28 but there is a God in heaven who reveals mysteries.

Romans 10:13
"Everyone who calls on the name of the Lord will be saved."

Chapter 36

Sleep

For those suffering from insomnia, fear of sleeping, or simple unable to sleep. Claim your sweet sleep through the word of God. It is effective; better than your sleeping pill.

> **Instructions:** All scriptures are taken from New International Version (NIV) Start reading every scripture out aloud with: ***"It is written......"***
>
> **SAMPLE VERSE:** - "The hands of Zerubbabel have laid the foundation of this temple; his hands will also complete it...."
> **Read Like This**
> It is written - "The hands of *(Your Name)* have laid the foundation of this temple; *(My)* hands will also complete it.... "

It is written..... Job 11:19
"You will lie down, with no one to make you afraid, and many will court your favor."

Psalm 4:8
"I will both lay me down in peace, and sleep: for thou, LORD, only makest me dwell in safety."

Proverbs 3:24
"when you lie down, you will not be afraid; when you lie down, your sleep will be sweet."

Job 3:13
"For now, I would be lying down in peace; I would be asleep and at rest"

Jeremiah 31:26
"At this I awoke and looked around. My sleep had been pleasant to me."

Psalm 3:5
"I lie down and sleep; I wake again, because the LORD sustains me."

Psalm 4:8
" I will lie down and sleep in peace, for you alone, O LORD, make me dwell in safety."

Jeremiah 20:11
11 But the LORD is with me like a mighty warrior; so my persecutors will stumble and not prevail.They will fail and be thoroughly disgraced; their dishonor will never be forgotten.

Galatians 5:10
10I am confident in the Lord that you will take no other view. The one who is throwing you into confusion will pay the penalty, whoever he may be.

Colossians 2:14
14having canceled the written code, with its regulations, that was against us and that stood opposed to us; he took it away, nailing it to the cross.

Colossians 2:15
15And having disarmed the powers and authorities, he made a public spectacle of them, triumphing over them by the cross.

Chapter 37

Sorrow

Sorrow is a spirit that can lead to depression. Talk to yourself through the word, and see the deliverance of your soul and mind through the word of God.

> **Instructions:** All scriptures are taken from New International Version (NIV) Start reading every scripture out aloud with: ***"It is written......"***
>
> **SAMPLE VERSE:** - "The hands of Zerubbabel have laid the foundation of this temple; his hands will also complete it...."
> **Read Like This**
> It is written - "The hands of *(Your Name)* have laid the foundation of this temple; *(My)* hands will also complete it.... "

It is written..... Psalm 42:11
"Why are you downcast, O my soul? Why so disturbed within me? Put your hope in God, for I will yet praise him, my Savior and my God."

1 Peter 4:7
"The end of all things is near. Therefore be clear minded and self-controlled so that you can pray."

2 Corinthians 12:9
"But he said to me, "My grace is sufficient for you, for my power is made perfect in weakness." Therefore I will boast all the more gladly about my weaknesses, so that Christ's power may rest on me."

2 Corinthians 9:8
"And God is able to make all grace abound to you, so that in all things at all times, having all that you need, you will abound in every good work."

Psalm 119:28
"My soul is weary with sorrow; strengthen me according to your word."

Isaiah 51:11
"The ransomed of the LORD will return. They will enter Zion with singing; everlasting joy will crown their heads. Gladness and joy will overtake them, and sorrow and sighing will flee away."

Isaiah 60:20
"Your sun will never set again, and your moon will wane no more; the LORD will be your everlasting light, and your days of sorrow will end."

Jeremiah 31:12
"They will come and shout for joy on the heights of Zion; they will rejoice in the bounty of the LORD; the grain, the new wine and the oil, the young of the flocks and herds. They will be like a well-watered garden, and they will sorrow no more."

Jeremiah 31:13
"Then maidens will dance and be glad, young men and old as well. I will turn their mourning into gladness; I will give them comfort and joy instead of sorrow."

Isaiah 53:4
"Surely he took up our infirmities and carried our sorrows, yet we considered him stricken by God, smitten by him, and afflicted."

Isaiah 35:10
" the ransomed of the LORD will return. They will enter Zion with singing; everlasting joy will crown their heads. Gladness and joy will overtake them, and sorrow and sighing will flee away."

2 Corinthians 7:10
"Godly sorrow brings repentance that leads to salvation and leaves no regret, but worldly sorrow brings death."

2 Corinthians 7:11
"See what this godly sorrow has produced in you: what earnestness, what eagerness to clear yourselves, what indignation, what alarm, what longing, what concern, what readiness to see justice done.
At every point you have proved yourselves to be innocent in this matter."

IT IS WRITTEN ... (YOUR SPIRITUAL SWORD & SHIELD)

Chapter 38

Spirits Leading And Direction

The will of God is supreme. You need to ask for the leading of God, and the best way to reason with God is through His own words. Ask and you shall receive according to what is written!

> **Instructions:** All scriptures are taken from New International Version (NIV) Start reading every scripture out aloud with: *"It is written......"*
>
> **SAMPLE VERSE:** - "The hands of Zerubbabel have laid the foundation of this temple; his hands will also complete it...."
> **Read Like This**
> It is written - "The hands of *(Your Name)* have laid the foundation of this temple; *(My)* hands will also complete it.... "

It is written..... **Psalm 31:3**
"Since you are my rock and my fortress, for the sake of your name lead and guide me."

Psalm 32:8
"I will instruct you and teach you in the way you should go; I will counsel you and watch over you."

Matthew 21:22
"If you believe, you will receive whatever you ask for in prayer."

Isaiah 42:16
"I will lead the blind by ways they have not known, along unfamiliar paths I will guide them; I will turn the darkness into light before them and make the rough places smooth. These are the things I will do; I will not forsake them."

Isaiah 58:11
"The LORD will guide you always; he will satisfy your needs in a sun-scorched land and will strengthen your frame. You will be like a well-watered garden, like a spring whose waters never fail."

Psalm 23:2
"He makes me lie down in green pastures, he leads me beside quiet waters"

Psalm 27:11
"Teach me your way, O LORD; lead me in a straight path because of my oppressors."

Psalm 31:3
"Since you are my rock and my fortress, for the sake of your name lead and guide me."

Psalm 61:2
"From the ends of the earth I call to you, I call as my heart grows faint; lead me to the rock that is higher than I."

Psalm 143:10
"Teach me to do your will, for you are my God; may your good Spirit lead me on level ground."

IT IS WRITTEN ... (YOUR SPIRITUAL SWORD & SHIELD)

Chapter 39

Spiritual Attack
(Fighting Back)

We are at war with the enemy. Stand tall and declare who you are to the enemy. Then send arrows through th word of God to demolish every stronghold and the enemy's place of hiding.

Instructions: All scriptures are taken from New International Version (NIV) Start reading every scripture out aloud with: **"It is written......"**

SAMPLE VERSE: - "The hands of Zerubbabel have laid the foundation of this temple; his hands will also complete it...."
Read Like This
It is written - "The hands of *(Your Name)* have laid the foundation of this temple; *(My)* hands will also complete it...."

It is written..... **Psalm 91:13**
"You will tread upon the lion and the cobra; you will trample the great lion and the serpent."

Psalm 34:19
"A righteous man may have many troubles, but the LORD delivers him from them all"

Psalm 34:7
"The angel of the LORD encamps around those who fear him, and he delivers them."

Psalm 44:5
"Through you we push back our enemies; through your name we trample our foes."

Psalm 18:34
"He trains my hands for battle; my arms can bend a bow of bronze."

Psalm 18:39
"You armed me with strength for battle; you made my adversaries bow at my feet."

Psalm 18:44
"As soon as they hear me, they obey me; foreigners cringe before me."

Psalm 18:45
"They all lose heart; they come trembling from their strongholds."

Psalm 23:5-6
5 "You prepare a table before me in the presence of my enemies. You anoint my head with oil;
my cup overflows.
6 Surely goodness and love will follow me all the days of my life, and I will dwell in the
house of the LORD forever.

Joshua 23:10
"One of you routs a thousand, because the LORD your God fights for you, just as he promised."

1 Samuel 17:45-46

45 ………….. "You come against me with sword and spear and javelin, but I come against you in the name of the LORD Almighty, the God of the armies of Israel, whom you have defied. 46 This day the LORD will hand you over to me, and I'll strike you down and cut off your head. Today ………………… the whole world will know that there is a God in Israel.

1 Samuel 17:47

"All those gathered here will know that it is not by sword or spear that the LORD saves; for the battle is the LORD's, and he will give all of you into our hands."

Psalm 7:15

"He who digs a hole and scoops it out falls into the pit he has made."

Numbers 23:23

"There is no sorcery against Jacob, no divination against Israel. It will now be said of Jacob and of Israel, 'See what God has done!'"

Deuteronomy 28:7

"The LORD will grant that the enemies who rise up against you will be defeated before you. They will come at you from one direction but flee from you in seven."

Psalm 118:11

"They surrounded me on every side, but in the name of the LORD I cut them off."

Isaiah 54:17
"no weapon forged against you will prevail, and you will refute every tongue that accuses you. This is the heritage of the servants of the LORD, and this is their vindication from me," declares the LORD."

Zechariah 4:7
"What are you, O mighty mountain? Before Zerubbabel you will become level ground. Then he will bring out the capstone to shouts of 'God bless it! God bless it!' "

Matthew 18:18
"I tell you the truth, whatever you bind on earth will be bound in heaven, and whatever you loose on earth will be loosed in heaven."

Matthew 7:19
"Every tree that does not bear good fruit is cut down and thrown into the fire."

Luke 3:9
"The axe is already at the root of the trees, and every tree that does not produce good fruit will be cut down and thrown into the fire."

Luke 10:19
"I have given you authority to trample on snakes and scorpions and to overcome all the power of the enemy; nothing will harm you."

Romans 10:13
"for, "Everyone who calls on the name of the Lord will be saved."

Romans 14:11
"It is written: " 'As surely as I live,' says the Lord, 'every knee will bow before me; every tongue will confess to God.'

Galatians 6:17
"Finally, let no one cause me trouble, for I bear on my body the marks of Jesus."

Philippians 2:10
"that at the name of Jesus every knee should bow, in heaven and on earth and under the earth"

1 Peter 1:23
"For you have been born again, not of perishable seed, but of imperishable, through the living and enduring word of God."

Psalm 20:7
"Some trust in chariots and some in horses, but we trust in the name of the LORD our God."

Leviticus 26:8
"Five of you will chase a hundred, and a hundred of you will chase ten thousand, and your enemies will fall by the sword before you."

Psalm 91:7
"A thousand may fall at your side, ten thousand at your right hand, but it will not come near you."

Deuteronomy 32:30
"How could one man chase a thousand, or two put ten thousand to flight, unless their Rock had sold them, unless the LORD had given them up?"

Chapter 40

Vision

The vision of God makes clear our purposes and His will for us. Seek through His word to know the vision of God and also to establish it firmly in your life.

> **Instructions:** All scriptures are taken from New International Version (NIV) Start reading every scripture out aloud with: ***"It is written......"***
>
> **SAMPLE VERSE:** - "The hands of Zerubbabel have laid the foundation of this temple; his hands will also complete it...."
> **Read Like This**
> It is written - "The hands of *(Your Name)* have laid the foundation of this temple; *(My)* hands will also complete it.... "

It is written..... Proverbs 29:18
"Where there is no revelation, the people cast off restraint; but blessed is he who keeps the law."

Isaiah 42:9
"See, the former things have taken place, and new things I declare; before they spring into being I announce them to you."

Jeremiah 29:11
"For I know the plans I have for you," declares the LORD, "plans to prosper you and not to harm you, plans to give you hope and a future."

Isaiah 52:11-12

11 "Depart, depart, go out from there! Touch no unclean thing! Come out from it and be pure, you who carry the vessels of the LORD.
12 But you will not leave in haste or go in flight; for the LORD will go before you, the God of Israel will be your rear guard.

Philippians 1:6

"being confident of this, that he who began a good work in you will carry it on to completion until the day of Christ Jesus"

Revelation 3:8

"I know your deeds. See, I have placed before you an open door that no one can shut. I know that you have little strength, yet you have kept my word and have not denied my name."

Habakkuk 2:2-3

2 Then the LORD replied: "Write down the revelation and make it plain on tablets so that a herald may run with it. 3 For the revelation awaits an appointed time; it speaks of the end and will not prove false. Though it linger, wait for it; it will certainly come and will not delay.

Daniel 8:19

" He said: "I am going to tell you what will happen later in the time of wrath, because the vision concerns the appointed time of the end. "

Ezekiel 12:24-25

24 For there will be no more false visions or flattering divinations among the people of Israel. 25 But I the LORD will speak what I will, and it shall be fulfilled without delay. For in your days, you rebellious house, I will fulfill whatever I say, declares the Sovereign LORD.' "

Hebrews 10:37-38

37For in just a very little while,
"He who is coming will come and will not delay.
38But my righteous one[a] will live by faith.
And if he shrinks back,
I will not be pleased with him."

2 Peter 3:9

"The Lord is not slow in keeping his promise, as some understand slowness. He is patient with you, not wanting anyone to perish, but everyone
to come to repentance."

IT IS WRITTEN ... (YOUR SPIRITUAL SWORD & SHIELD)

A SAMPLE PRAYER USING SCRIPTURES VERSES

A Heart towards God
Prepare your mind and heart to stand in the presence of God in total focus and concentration. No disturbances and if there are ignore them!

Father it is written in your word that .. *"**May the words of my mouth and the meditation of my heart be pleasing in your sight, O LORD, my Rock and my Redeemer." - Psalm 19:14.*** Let therefore, my thoughts and meditation be pleasing to you today, and in this hour; Father, I ask in Jesus name.

Thanksgiving and Worship
Give God a deep felt and sincere thanks giving from your heart. You will feel His presence when your worship is in sincerity and truth.

Seek Forgiveness and Cleansing from all Sins.
Father it is written in your word that .. you are *"**compassionate and gracious, slow to anger, abounding in love. ⁹ He will not always accuse, nor will he harbor his anger forever; ¹⁰ he does not treat us as our sins deserve or repay us according to our iniquities."*** **(Psalm 103:8-10)** your nature is compassionate and your love upon me will never cease.

You have promised that you will never treat me according to what my sins deserve, and that is why I come before you for forgiveness today. Lord, I do confess that I am a sinner, for I was born in sin. I ask you Lord, to forgive those sins that I committed that are errors in the kingdom.

It is written **"Who can discern his errors? Forgive my hidden faults."**-(Psalm 19:12) Lord, I seek cleansing from all these sin today. *It is written in your word that I* **" have redemption through the blood of Jesus, and the forgiveness of sins, in accordance with the riches of God's grace"** in my life (Ephesians 1:7)

I plead the blood of Jesus to cleanse me from all sin, and I will be made whole according to your word; **"Purge me with hyssop (the blood of Jesus), and I shall be clean; Wash me, and I shall be whiter than snow."** (Psalm 51:7)

Lord, I thank you because you have heard me and have purged me clean. Thank you, because I am able to stand in your holy presence at this time.

Establish Your authority
Bring forth before God scriptures that will establish your authority, and your right to be in His court. Look up the words of God that promises that the angels and heaven must move on your behalf.

Lord, I thank you for the authority I have in Christ Jesus. *It is written in your word that* **"you have given (me) authority to trample on snakes and scorpions and to overcome all the power of the enemy; nothing will harm (me)"**. (Luke 10:19)

Use the Authority
I take hold of this authority that you have given me, and I go to the root of my problem or affliction. According to your word, it says in **Luke 3:9** *"The axe is already at the root of the trees, and every tree that does not produce good fruit will be cut down and thrown into the fire."*

With authority, I command the axe of God to begin to go to the root source of (my affliction). You tree of barrenness, you are not bearing any good fruit in me, so you must go. Axe of God, CUT IT DOWN from the root in the name of Jesus and cast it into fire. Holy Ghost fire, burn the uprooted tree up in Jesus's name.

Decree Unto the Enemy
Satan it is written that I *"I will tread upon the lion and the cobra; I will trample the great lion and the serpent."*- (**Psalm 91:13**) you are that serpent and the lion. I tread upon you in the name of Jesus. I call the Holy Ghost fire to crush you, so that you will no longer rise again in my life. In every area of my life where you afflicted, hear the word of God. Since I already have forgiveness of sin in my life, you do not have any legal right to torment me. It is written that *"As soon as you hear me, you MUST obey me; all you foreigners must cringe before me."*(**Psalm 18:44**)

Every word I speak now in the name of Jesus must be obeyed. In the name of Jesus, I command you to remove every demon on mission in my life. I command the fire of God to burn every weapon you have fashioned against me etc............

Cancel every weapon and gathering by fire
I cancel every word spoken against me in any realm. I call on

the fire of God to scatter you where ever you have gather to talk evil; make evil plans, against my life, my home and my marriage; *for it is written....*

"Take counsel together, and it shall come to naught; speak the word, and it shall not stand: for God is with us." (Isaiah 8:10).

As it is written so shall it be. Your words will have no effect on me and any words that have been having effective before is hereby removed and the peace of God shall reign there.

THIS IS ONLY A SAMPLE PRAYER

DEVISE YOUR OWN PRAYER ACCORDING TO YOUR NEEDS AND AFFLICTION.

The point of this prayer sample is to help you to see the way to arrange your argument with the help of the scripture verses and the inspiration of the Holy Spirit.. This prayer is not the set law. Speak to God in your own phrases and He will hear you. He knows you best.

SHALOM

ABOUT THE AUTHORS

Dammy Olanrewaju Owen

Called to be an Apostle of Jesus Christ, sent both to the Body of Christ and the unbelievers. He is the Founder and General Overseer of the two Ministries.
World Evangelism and Salvation Ministry Inc. which started in December 15th, 2000. The ministry is currently 9 years in anniversary with 8 local churches in Nigeria.

Apostle Owen on the directive of God handed over the role of the Senior Pastor to concentrate solely on Evangelical work, and the ministry **World Evangelism Outreach Ministry Inc.** took off in August 2003 conducting Crusades, Revivals and Church revivals in several cities and States in the West African Countries, South Africa and The United States.

The vision and Mission of this ministry is preaching the word of God undiluted with concentration on *Holiness, Salvation, Healing and Deliverance.*

Several local churches have joined hands to come together to have Apostle Dammy Owen conduct crusades to preach salvation, healing and deliverance.

He also holds a **Telephone Conference Prayer Vigil** *(Total Transformation Phone Conference)* for those who needs to continue in fervent prayers to perfect their healing and deliverance for people from everywhere. people from the USA, England, Germany and Canada. have been calling in to join the prayer line.

In the planning works is a *Fire Faith Center* that will be based in Maryland or in its environs. The clinic will serve to minister to cases of individuals whose deliverance and healing according to the leading of the spirit are serious and cannot not be resolved in a day during crusades or church service ministrations; such cases requires specific instructions from God added with close monitoring to complete their healing and deliverance.

Apostle Dammy Owen is married with children and resides in Maryland, USA.

For more information about his ministry,
please visit the website
www.weomi.org

ABOUT THE AUTHORS

Olabisi Oluyemisi Odubanjo

Called to be a prophet and a teacher of Jesus Christ; sent both to Body of Christ. She is the founder of several Ministries: **Brother Keepers International Ministries Inc.** A Mission ministry whose vision is to bring forth the righteousness of God unto the aids victims and their children in Africa, transforming the lives of the poor in the US and Africa and its environs.

Ministers of Christ Resource Network (MCRN); a ministry to train and provide resources for those whom God has called into Ministry; teaching them to activate their spiritual gifts and power in the kingdom of God.

Elohiym Publishing House Inc. a ministry to bring forth, proclaiming and broadcasting the knowledge of the kingdom of God and all its principles on this earth. The ministry has produced several books for the body of Christ. This book is a product of the ministry.

Endtime Revivalist Ministries. This ministry is a prophetic Ministry that holds prophetic conferences in healing and deliverance all over the United States. Prophet Bisi is also a music Minister who brings forth the presence of God powerfully, creating an atmosphere for God's miraculous; during their prophetic worship conferences and concerts.

Prophet Olabisi Odubanjo resides in Maryland with her family.

OTHER BOOKS BY APOSTLE DAMMY OWEN

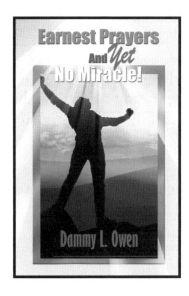

Earnest Prayers yet No Miracle!
By:
Dammy Lanre Owen

Maintaining and Retaining your divine miracle to perfection
Paper Back, pages 104

USD $10.00
Canada $12.00
(plus shipping and handling)

There are many believers who have been earnestly praying for healing, deliverance and breakthroughs for years; and yet they have not been able to attain their miracle. Many such Christians have been afflicted by demonic forces, that they cannot seem to overcome. Many have been waiting on God for so many years; when all they needed was the right information and understanding of the problem, using the right spiritual weapons and their victory would come easily through the power of God.

Apostle Dammy Owen has provided in this book, the information you need to end the years of waiting, so you can achieve the desired result in prayer.

GET A COPY TODAY.
WWW.SPIRITSELECT.COM
WW.WEOMI.ORG
OR CALL 1-(800) 270-9894

IT IS WRITTEN ... (YOUR SPIRITUAL SWORD & SHIELD)

NOTES

Jot down more scriptures as you find them in your daily bible reading. That way, you can remember them to refer to them when you need them.

OTHER BOOKS BY
APOSTLE DAMMY OWEN

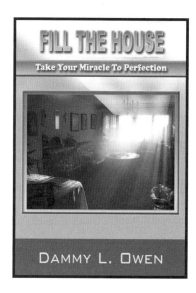

Fill The House
By:
Dammy Lanre Owen

Maintaining and Retaining your divine miracle to perfection

Paper Back,

USD $10.00
Canada $12.00
(plus shipping and handling)

The word of God says that when an evil spirit leaves the human body; it roams about for a while. Finding no abode it attempts to come back to its old house. If it finds the house empty, it will re-enter; with seven worse friends, and the state of that person will be seven times worse of, than when he or she received the deliverance or healing.

Deliverance is easy, however, maintaining your miracle to complete wholeness is harder. This book will give you all the guidelines you need to make your freedom and victory permanent in the Lord, and in Jesus☐ name.

GET A COPY TODAY.
WWW.SPIRITSELECT.COM
WW.WEOMI.ORG
OR CALL 1-(800) 270-9894

NOTES

Jot down more scriptures as you find them in your daily bible reading. That way, you can remember them to refer to them when you need them.

NOTES

Jot down more scriptures as you find them in your daily bible reading. That way, you can remember them to refer to them when you need them.

NOTES

NOTES

Jot down more scriptures as you find them in your daily bible reading. That way, you can remember them to refer to them when you need them.

IT IS WRITTEN ... (YOUR SPIRITUAL SWORD & SHIELD)

NOTES

IT IS WRITTEN ... (YOUR SPIRITUAL SWORD & SHIELD)

NOTES

Jot down more scriptures as you find them in your daily bible reading. That way, you can remember them to refer to them when you need them.

NOTES